Praise for *The Parent's Guide*

• •

"Shawn Edgington's book is a must-have for parents in this digital age. While there are many benefits to using social media, there are also very real potential dangers, such as online predators, cyberbullying, identity theft, and more. *The Parent's Guide to Texting, Facebook, and Social Media* helps parents equip their children to protect themselves and their personal information."

—**Spencer Christian**
Weather anchor for ABC7 News (San Francisco) and cohost of
View from the Bay, former weather anchor of *Good Morning America*

"Teens face a number of significant challenges when using technology and parents are charged with educating their children about the safe and responsible use of a variety of digital devices and online environments. *The Parent's Guide to Texting, Facebook, and Social Media* equips parents with the tools and resources they need to encourage the appropriate use of computers and cell phones."

—**Justin Patchin,** PhD
Codirector of the Cyberbullying Research Center
Coauthor of *Bullying Beyond the Schoolyard: Preventing and Responding to Cyberbullying*

"I believe it is so important for books just like *The Parent's Guide to Texting, Facebook, and Social Media* to be available to help educate and bring parents up to speed on the world that our children live in today."

—**Tina Meier**
Mother and founder of The Megan Meier Foundation

"Taekwon-Do and other types of martial arts are not really about punching and kicking; they're about developing survival skills. In today's digital environment, it's never been more important to teach our children the survival skills they need to know while they are using social media. *The Parent's Guide* gives parents the tools to help us empower our kids to develop the skills they need to survive and thrive."

—**Master Gordon Jue**
seventh-degree black belt, US vice president
International Taekwon-Do Federation

"*The Parent's Guide* teaches parents why they must be proactive and not reactive in order to stop the online harassment and cyberbullying of their children that begins in sixth grade. Don't look the other way. Know the facts; knowledge is power. We can help our children and students most by dealing with issues directly, not by providing justification or excuses."

—**Kevin Johnson**
Senior director, Pleasanton Unified School District, California

"Responding to the needs of our children is essential and requires that parents meet them where they spend their time. Shawn's book provides parents with the skills and knowledge to navigate through the world of texting, Facebook, and other social media with the purpose of understanding the world in which our children are communicating, working, and learning."

—**Christopher L. Shaffer**
Principal, Pottsgrove High School, Pennsylvania

"As both the chief of the Oakland School Police and as a father, I know firsthand how important it is to understand both the benefits and the dangers to children in today's world of rapidly evolving technology and social networking. Shawn Edgington has written the blueprint for creating healthy boundaries for children around technology."

—**Pete Sarna**
Chief of Police, Oakland School Police in California

"This is a must-read for the responsible parent of any tech-savvy kid. Shawn shares her vast knowledge on the way youth communicate today."

—NJ Frank
Film producer, *Submit: The Reality of Cyberbullying*

"This book should be handed out to all parents as their children start kindergarten. It's well written, informative, and a little scary. Shawn reaches into a world that very few parents I come in contact with are aware of. Every teacher, school counselor, and principal should be required to read this book."

Debbie Johnson
Bookstore manager

"In an era when we are scrambling to keep up with the pace of technology, it is important to also understand the boundaries. Shawn Edgington has emerged as an essential voice for parents and tech-obsessed kids in our rapidly changing world."

Samantha Ettus
Bestselling author, TV personality, personal branding expert, and mom of three

"Today's reality is that students of all ages communicate virtually through mobile and online resources and it is imperative that parents understand how to protect their children in this environment. Shawn's book helps parents identify the danger zones and gives direction on how to provide guidance and protection. This guidance is imperative in a context where communication and information fly and emotions can escalate quickly if not controlled and managed. It is a spectacular overview of how to work within today's social media to keep your children safe."

—Jeremy Konko
President and founder of GuestAssist

"Shawn is the ultimate expert on teens and texting. She has been a guest on our show many times, and each time she provides our listeners with invaluable tips and advice on texting and teens. Shawn has all the tools parents need to keep their kids safe in cyber world. What's more, she is in the know and up-to-date on the latest and greatest strides in social networks and media. Thank you, Shawn, for your hard work and indispensable insight!"

—**Maura Ridder**
Attorney and radio show host and producer

"*The Parent's Guide* is a valuable resource that helps parents gain a better understanding of what they need to know to in order to survive in the twenty-first century. In my line of work, awareness and observation are the keys to online safety. In order for our children to stay safe online, parents and guardians need to provide protection to today's youth by being aware and involved in how children are using social media and understanding that it's important to take advantage of free resources like ComputerCOP, available at your local law enforcement office."

—**Stephen DelGiorno**
President and creator, ComputerCOP

"I remember my parents refusing to buy a TV for fear that it would take over my brain. Today's social media versus the 60s black-and-white TV is like comparing a bedtime story to an X-rated movie. When your child adds Facebook, Twitter, and a mobile phone to their social entourage, they've just added a couple of hundred million bidirectional channels including sex, evil, and an endless "spend" account that you haven't got a clue about. *The Parents Guide to Texting, Facebook and Social Media* clues you in and teaches you how take control like it's a black-and-white TV."

—**Peter Jackson**
Silicon Valley CEO

The Parent's Guide to Texting, Facebook, and Social Media

Understanding the **Benefits** and **Dangers** of Parenting in a Digital World

. . . .

Shawn Marie Edgington

Author of *Read Between the Lines*
and Creator of the One-Click Safety Series

Brown Books Publishing Group
Dallas, Texas

The Parent's Guide to Texting, Facebook, and Social Media Understanding the Benefits and Dangers of Parenting in a Digital World

Brown Books Publishing Group
16250 Knoll Trail, Suite 205
brownbooks.com
(972) 381-0009

A New Era in Publishing.™

ISBN 978-1-934812-97-6
Library of Congress Control Number 2010942815

Cover art by Margaret Gockel

Printed in the United States of America
10 9 8 7 6 5 4 3 2 1

For special sales or to learn more about the author, please visit www.ShawnEdgington.com.

For additional resources, including the One-Click Safety Kit, the One-Click Audio Series, and information on Shawn's first book, *Read Between the Lines*, visit www.ShawnEdgington.com.

• •

Dedicated to my mother,
Patricia Dolan, for being the best
mother a girl could ever dream of.

And to Nicole, David, and Derek.
Thank you for your support,
patience, and belief in me.
I love you all.

• •

Contents

Foreword

My name is Tina Meier, the founder and executive director of the Megan Meier Foundation. Many of you may have heard the name Megan Meier through many different media outlets, or maybe you have never heard her name at all. Megan is my daughter, and believe me when I tell you that she was a spitfire from the day I gave birth to her on November 6, 1992.

Megan's elementary and middle school years had many bumps along the way, including a diagnosis of depression and attention deficit disorder, as well as a constant battle with name-calling. Mean-spirited names such as "fat cow" and "elephant" bothered Megan to the point that she stopped eating lunch because she was so embarrassed. Girls found her in the gym locker-room crying because she was being laughed at and called "thunder thighs."

Megan was getting ready to turn fourteen years old when she asked if she could have a MySpace account. I wasn't too thrilled about it but I told her she could if she adhered to the following five rules: Megan didn't have the password to her account, I did. Her profile had to be kept to private. I had to approve all of the content and pictures that were put on her MySpace page. Computers were always in open spaces in the house, never allowed in her bedroom. I had a program that monitored every instant message and web page that Megan was on.

Yes, I was a very protective mother. You see, I was worried about the sexual predators that roam the pages of social networking sites and prey on young teens.

Believe me, Megan wasn't thrilled by all the rules, but she wanted a MySpace account badly enough that she accepted them. Megan started adding her friends from her old school and her new friends. Approximately three weeks later, Megan received a friend request from a boy named Josh Evans. She thought he was so "hot" and asked me if she could accept him as a friend. I told her that she could, but if he said anything negative or sexual, he would be deleted immediately.

Yes, I know—how could I let Megan add someone that she didn't know, right? I wanted to make sure that she didn't go to another computer, make up a different MySpace profile, and add him without my knowledge.

Josh offered Megan all of the things that she never heard from a boy her age: "you're beautiful," you have "beautiful eyes" and a "great smile," and so on. This went on for five weeks and Megan told me that Josh liked her and she liked him. I would say, "Megan, how can you have a relationship with someone online when you don't even know who they really are? They could be a ten-year-old child playing a game or a forty-year-old sexual predator." Megan would laugh at me and put her hands in the air and say, "Mom, please, I know him."

October 15, 2006: Megan was finishing up her birthday invitations and asked if she could get on MySpace. I signed her on and she looked puzzled and said, "Mom, Josh sent me a message saying he didn't want to be friends with me anymore and that no one likes me."

October 16, 2006: I picked Megan up from school and she said, "Mom, everyone is coming to my party and it's going to be so great!" When we arrived home, Megan asked if she could get on MySpace to see if Josh had responded, which he had. His message said, "You heard me. No one likes you and I don't want to be friends with you anymore."

Megan was confused and asked him, "What are you talking about and where are you getting this from?" They went back and forth for approximately ten minutes until I told Megan that it was time to sign off because I had to leave.

Things quickly went from bad to worse. I left my house to take my younger daughter to the orthodontist and when I returned home, I found Megan at the computer, sobbing. I asked her to get up and let me see what was going on. Messages, bulletins, and comments were running rampant on MySpace between Megan, Josh, and now two other girls who had gotten involved. The messages ranged from "You're not a nice person," to vulgar, hurtful, and downright mean words.

I said to Megan, "You're not the things that they are calling you." She responded, "Who's going to believe me? They're going to tell everyone at my school." I said,

"Megan, you should have listened and signed off when I told you to and we could have handled this differently. Now this has turned into a war." Megan looked at me with tears in her eyes and said, "You're supposed to be my mom. You're supposed to be on my side," and ran off to her room.

It had been about twenty minutes when all of a sudden I had this horrible feeling run through my body and I took off to Megan's room upstairs. I opened her door and found my baby hanging lifelessly from her closet. I screamed for her dad and he ran up the stairs, frantically grabbed Megan down, and started giving her CPR as I called 911. Megan was transported to the hospital the evening of October 16, 2006, in a coma, and passed away on October 17, 2006—just weeks shy of her fourteenth birthday.

It is the worst possible feeling to hold your child as they take their last breath. We left the hospital in complete shock thinking, *This didn't just happen. This has to be a dream.*

For the next five weeks, we walked in a fog, trying to get through each day and asking ourselves, *Why did this happen? What did we miss or not do?* But there were no answers.

It was Thanksgiving weekend when I received a call from a neighbor down the street who I didn't know very well. She said, "Tina, I have some information about Megan's death and I need you and Ron to come to a meeting this morning."

When we arrived at the meeting, we were informed that Josh Evans, the boy that Megan had talked with for five weeks on the Internet, was a fake person. It was really Lori Drew, a forty-seven-year-old mom who lived four houses down the street, her daughter, Sarah Drew, who was thirteen years old and had been friends with Megan since the fourth grade, and an eighteen-year-old girl named Ashley Grills who worked part-time for Lori.

The reason they created this fake MySpace account was to see if Megan was talking about Sarah Drew behind her back because they heard that Megan had called her a bad name. Megan and Sarah's friendship had its ups and downs during seventh grade and finally dissipated the summer prior to eighth grade. If you are sitting there shaking your head at all of this, believe me, I still do—even as I'm typing this today.

This is why I believe it is so important for books like *The Parent's Guide to Texting, Facebook, and Social Media* to be available to help educate and bring parents up to speed on the world that our children live in today.

Today, I travel throughout the country as a keynote speaker, giving presentations on Megan's story, bullying, and cyberbullying to kindergarten through twelfth grade schools, youth rallies, Internet safety summits, parent/educator programs, and professional organizations. I speak nationally and internationally on many network television stations, news magazines, and syndicated talk shows.

If you would like more information about the Megan Meier Foundation or would like to donate to help the Foundation continue its mission, please visit: www.MeganMeierFoundation.org.

Thank you,

Tina Meier

Mother and founder of the Megan Meier Foundation

Introduction

Dear Fellow Parent,

The Parent's Guide was inspired by my first book, *Read Between the Lines,* and a personal and difficult situation that occurred with my teenage daughter. She was harassed via text messages and cyberbullied on Facebook for months. At the time, there weren't any solutions to help a parent deal with and defend against these types of difficult situations.

As the CEO of a national insurance firm, I manage risk and prevent loss for business clients around the country. That said, you can imagine the surprise and level of desperation I felt when my teenage daughter was harassed, threatened, and bullied for months . . . and I had no idea how to help her. Nothing I came up with worked.

I know how helpless it feels *not* to know what to do or where to turn when technology is being used to threaten your child, because that is exactly how I felt when my daughter was the target of online bullies.

That was two years ago. Since then, I've interviewed thousands of teens and spoken to hundreds of parents about virtual harassment. These discussions led me to write this book and create the One-Click Safety Kit and the One-Click Audio Series.

I get asked by parents and professionals to speak about my books and programs focusing on how to defend against online harassment, sexting prevention, and cyberbullying. I'm also asked to talk about the benefits of using technology to communicate with coworkers, family, and friends. I'm fortunate to be featured on countless television and radio programs across the nation to discuss the pros and cons of living in a digital world and how to avoid one-click nightmares.

It's my mission to help families everywhere understand the proactive measures that must be taken to minimize their children's exposure to the hazards of growing up totally connected in a digital world.

Now it's up to you. Take my advice and make use of the tools that this book has to offer. It was written from personal experience, professional knowledge, research, and advice from professionals in the field of safety and loss prevention.

I'm confident that by reading *The Parent's Guide*, you'll have a better understanding about online and textual harassment, sexting, and the benefits and dangers of parenting in a digital world.

You'll find free resources for parents, information about my first book, *Read Between the Lines*, The One-Click Safety Kit, and the One-Click Audio Series at www.ShawnEdgington.com.

Sincerely,

Shawn Edgington

1

· ·

A One-Click Nightmare

Parenting isn't easy. The truth is, parenting has never been trouble-free, but today's generation might be the most difficult generation that parents have ever had to face. With the explosion of the Internet, the text-addiction that has taken over our teens' lives, and the development of social media such as MySpace, World of Warcraft, Facebook, and YouTube, the levels of complication for parenting around technology has hit an all-time high.

The majority of today's parents weren't raised on computers. You might have taken a computer class in school, but today's teens are playing games online and on cell phones by the time they are age two, and the lucky ones are learning to develop web pages in elementary and middle school. The majority of our children have cell phones, access to the Internet, and belong to social networking sites that are changing the way they will interact forever.

Do you often wonder why today's teens have to be connected with their fifteen "BFFs" at the same time? The truth is, it's how they communicate, live, and socialize. Their technology is their "everything." Parenting in today's digital world isn't easy, but if you're proactive, get involved, and attempt to understand your child's online life, you're much closer to avoiding a one-click nightmare.

Online Dangers

Bullying and sexual predators are not new evils for parents. The fact is that bad people who prey on the innocent have been around for generations. But, now that children and adult predators can use technology to target their prey, the schoolyard bully and the sexual predator have more power and reach than they ever did before. It's disturbing to know that:

➢ About half of all teenagers have experienced some form of online harassment (Cyberbullying Research Center).

➢ 37 percent of teens admit to using social networking sites to victimize and harass their peers (TheExaminer.com).

➢ 43 percent of teens use their cell phones to say insulting things to others (LG Mobile Phones).

➢ 64 percent of all teens say they do things online they don't want their parents to know about (Lenhart, Madden, and Rainie, 2006).

➢ 71 percent of teens receive messages online from strangers (National Center for Missing and Exploited Children).

➤ 51 percent of teens have been asked for personal information online (McAfee Inc.).

➤ 83 percent of teens admit to texting in the middle of the night (LG Mobile Phones).

➤ 45 percent of teens admit to texting and driving (LG Mobile Phones).

➤ 30 percent of teens contemplate meeting a person they met online (Teenage Research Unlimited).

➤ 42 percent of youths ages ten to seventeen have seen Internet porn in the past year. Two-thirds of these exposures were unwanted (University of New Hampshire's Crimes Against Children Research Center).

What's Your Biggest Nightmare?

It's a fact that every parent has their own nightmares about what could happen to their child online. What's *your* biggest nightmare?

➤ Your eight-year-old daughter receives a solicitation by text message for a naked photo of herself from her eight-year-old schoolmate.

➤ Your daughter's best friend is cutting herself and no one knows she's doing it except for her Facebook "friends," because that's where she's bragging about it.

➤ Your twelve-year-old son posts a "Termination List" on Facebook that includes the top ten people he would like to see wiped off of the planet.

➤ Your fourteen-year-old son asks his fourteen-year-old girlfriend for a nude photo and his request is granted. He receives the photo by text and then posts it to his Facebook site for everyone to see. Is he now a distributor of pornography?

➤ Your fifteen-year-old daughter is pregnant and you don't know it, but her Facebook "friends" do.

➤ Your seventeen-year-old son is the leader of a group of children who target their schoolmates (who don't fit in) on Facebook, MySpace, and FormSpring.

➤ Your thirteen-year-old son is being harassed by text and online because he's gay.

➤ Your seventeen-year-old son is involved in setting up a threatening, racist MySpace profile about a fellow student that contains white supremacist-type comments.

➤ Your fifteen-year-old son has received more than 15,000 threatening text messages over a two-month period. He can't take it anymore and commits suicide.

➤ Your thirteen-year-old daughter "friended" a forty-five-year old stranger and is now missing.

➤ Your sixteen-year-old son is being made fun of on Facebook every day because of his special needs.

➤ Your fifteen-year-old daughter gets on the wrong side of the "in crowd" and that escalates into nonstop text and Facebook harassment over four months from multiple mean girls.

➤ Your sixteen-year-old daughter has her naked photo forwarded by text message to the entire school by her ex-boyfriend. Two weeks later, she takes her own life.

➤ Your fourteen-year-old son texts a death threat to a girl who turned him down to the homecoming dance.

Parent's Guide Fact: These examples of online behaviors aren't necessarily factual, but they easily could be.

Do you think this couldn't happen to your child? Think again! Do you think there's nothing you can do to avoid these types of situations from occurring in your home? You're wrong. When it comes to parenting around technology, your first step is to become a defensive parent.

Back in the day, the bullies at school used to threaten you or beat you up on the playground or in the parking lot. Today, the cyberbully can torment your child anywhere and at any time. The power of technology gives bullies the ability to reach out to their targets with ease. Think of it as a bully on steroids.

Consider this: One of your ex-friends called you a slut on Facebook and posted a picture of you in a bikini she had dug up from a pool party. Within minutes, friends, strangers, and peers had agreed with your new nickname by clicking the "Like" icon or by adding additional comments such as "I agree; she stole my boyfriend!" or "What a loser—she cuts school all the time" or "I heard she does drugs" all within a few hours, and all of this is happening right in front of your eyes. The next day, you have to walk into school with what feels like a scarlet letter tattooed to your forehead. **What would you do?**

There's no easy answer. Today's youth are finding themselves falling victim to the perils of social and mobile networking hazards at an alarming rate. Humiliation, cyberbullying, textual harassment, sexting, lack of morality, and bad behavior online has become the norm for teens. According to recent surveys:

➢ Over half of bullying and cyberbully attacks go unreported to parents, educators, or authorities.[*]

➢ On a daily average, 160,000 children miss school because they fear they will be bullied if they attend classes.[*]

➢ On a monthly average, 282,000 students are physically attacked by a bully each month.[*]

➢ Every seven minutes a child is bullied on a school playground, with over 85 percent of those instances occurring without any intervention.[*]

➢ 50 percent of teens admit to being bullied online or by text message.[*]

➢ As a result of being bullied, 19,000 children are attempting suicide over the course of one year.[*]

➢ Once every half hour a child commits suicide as a direct result of being bullied.[*]

[*]*According to the International Adoption Articles Directory*

With the high-profile teen suicides that have been reported nationally as a result of being cyberbullied, there's no way to turn a blind eye to this problem. Situations like these happen every day in the news and on the radio, but the majority go unreported. Reputations are getting ruined, children are getting beaten up, and some are dying. What we need are parents to open their eyes and realize that it's time to start taking responsibility for what their children are doing online.

The New Schoolyard Bully

Online harassment and cyberbullying is more effective than ever. Bad people can easily connect with their targets hundreds of times a day. Social networks are like virtual stages that online bullies can use to reach out and threaten or harass whenever they choose. The top six reasons virtual harassment has become the choice of today's bullies are:

- ➢ Technology is portable and easy to access
- ➢ It's persistent and instantly harmful
- ➢ Content can be edited and altered
- ➢ It's distributed with lightening speed and breadth
- ➢ There is a lack of accountability
- ➢ It's insidious and dangerous

It's now more common that physical fights are a direct result of harassment or threats that originated in the virtual world or by text message. Sometimes, children are harassed and tormented for weeks or months before the physical fight occurs.

*A **Parent's Guide** Story Submission: "I was harassed and threatened by text and online for months for standing up for what I believed in. One night after a football game, a gang of girls at my school who had been harassing me threatened to destroy my car and my life and then confronted me at our local hamburger hangout. I was lucky that night, because two older men witnessed what was about to happen and saved me. I never told my parents or even my best friend what was happening to me because I was embarrassed."*

Because our generation wasn't raised on computers, we tend to think how ridiculous cyberbullying and textual harassment sounds. Should this *really* be a major concern? Fathers are usually the first to say, "I taught my son to stand up for himself using his fists. Who cares what happens on Facebook or YouTube?"

What parents don't realize is that technology has changed the way the typical schoolyard bully now attacks their prey. Now, bullies use powerful social networking sites to humiliate and destroy their target's reputation *first* . . . long before a schoolyard fight takes place.

Unlike most adults, children don't separate technology from the rest of their lives. Their everyday life and their digital life are one and the same, with a constant flow of information exchanging between the two. Total connectivity almost guarantees your child will be involved in an act of cyberbullying—in one form or another.

If nothing else, parents must accept the fact that technology-based threats are a reality, and it's difficult for children to escape the threats of an online bully. The answer lies with teaching our children how to handle these types of situations when they arise. The most important thing parents can do is commit to parenting around technology and take the defensive measures necessary to show their children how to defend against online attacks.

Parents' Roles and Responsibilities

You need to have honest, open, and ongoing conversations with your children about how cyberbullies attack others and why it's important that you stay involved to help get them through difficult situations. Let your children know that these are the only reasons you will be monitoring their cell phones and social networking sites. Assure them it's not because you are interested in their personal information, but that you need to be there in case they get caught in a difficult online situation that they don't know how to handle.

Your first thought when it comes to monitoring social media might be: "Watching over my child's shoulder is prying into their personal life and is none of my business." I know, because it's also how I felt. Had I been doing my job—doing regular "checkups" on my daughter's Facebook account—I would have known immediately how bad the abuse had been for her.

An important note about monitoring: Don't become a cyberstalker or a cell phone spy by going on your children's sites or by scrolling through their text messages without their knowledge. If you do, you risk having your child lose trust in you, which could ruin your relationship forever. Instead, take the following measures to defend against online harassment:

- ➢ Set up a Google Alert for your child's name and make sure to set the content filter to "strict" and include "all online searches."

- ➢ Set clear user boundaries and discuss what the consequences would be for misuse of any technology. You can accomplish this by executing the "Cell Phone and Social Media Contract"— often referred to as the "Rules of Engagement"— which is located in the back of this book.

- ➢ Regularly and openly monitor all social media accounts until your child is mature enough to socialize online without supervision.

- ➢ Obey the age limits that social networking sites have set for users.

- ➢ Empower your children to Ignore/Block/Report.

- ➢ Online image protection, damage control, and proactive content monitoring are your parental obligation and responsibility.

- ➢ Be prepared to restrict mobile devices or Internet privileges when necessary.

- ➢ Don't be sneaky when monitoring—be up-front and honest about what you're doing and how you're doing it.

- ➢ Teach your children to have respect for others online and by text.

➢ Advocate and attend school programs that provide education and awareness about their social media policies, procedures, and programs.

A Parent's Guide Story Submission: "I set up a Google Alert for my son's name a year ago. I just received a notification from Google, and upon doing further research, I found out that one of his friends had posted a video that made him look like a racist and a homophobe. I was successful in getting it removed pretty quickly thanks to the notification from my Google Alert."

What age should you start talking to your children about the "Rules of Engagement"? Only you know what's right for your child—just be sure you don't forget to have the conversation before your child goes online alone or when they get the gift of their first mobile device.

Parent's Guide Fact: Start talking with children about the "Rules of Engagement" before they get their first cell phone and before you allow them to start networking online.

Teach Them to Think Before They Click

From day one, teach your child to be digitally aware, to protect their online image, and to come to you right away if anything goes wrong. Open communication and proactive steps are critical in trying to protect your children from cyberbullying and harassment by text, the fastest growing forms of bullying today. Remind them:

1. Assume a webcam is always on.

2. Nothing that is said or done online is private.

3. What's posted on the Internet stays on the Internet forever.

4. Videos and pictures cannot be deleted once they are posted.

5. School admissions officers, coaches, friends, and potential employers are using Facebook as part of their background checking process.

6. His or her image is absolutely worth protecting.

A **Parent's Guide** *Story Submission: "I texted my boyfriend a picture of myself in just my bra, lying down on my bed in a sexy position. Thinking back, I knew I shouldn't have done it, but he asked so I felt like I had to. He loved it, so I sent him more. When we broke up, he posted them on Facebook for* everyone *to see. I was humiliated and wanted to change schools."*

The Consequences of a Mis-Click

If there's one thing children are completely attached to and in their minds "can't live without," it's their cell phones. Parents everywhere have testified that restricting their teen's cell phone and Internet access works well as a consequence for inappropriate use.

Typically parents don't take the phone away, as they still want to have the ability to contact their child. A great tool for limiting the bells and whistles that come with almost every cell phone is the parental controls feature that is available for a low monthly fee from your wireless provider. This allows you to choose what feature(s) you are going to restrict or take away, while still leaving the ability to make and receive calls intact.

*A **Parent's Guide** Story Submission: "I regularly monitor my fifteen-year-old daughter's Facebook account. During one of my regular Facebook reviews, I noticed my daughter had posted a totally inappropriate comment saying she couldn't wait to wear her boyfriend's new football jersey with the number sixty-nine on it. I immediately sent her a text and asked her to delete her post. It could have been an innocent comment (or not), but I know it's my job to protect her online image."*

The most important thing is to discuss the consequences for inappropriate or abusive cell phone or Internet use before you agree to purchase or upgrade their cell phone, pay for their monthly service, or allow access to the Internet. Be sure to set the usage rules, and then follow through with the consequences. One without the other is useless.

The One-Click Safety Kit

If you find yourself needing a turnkey "Rules of Engagement" program to help your children avoid online dangers and help you negotiate with your children *before* they get access to technology (or continue to get access), the One-Click Safety Kit is the solution you've been looking for. Here's what you get:

➢ Cell Phone and Social Media Contract—The "Rules of Engagement" provides twenty talking points about the dos and don'ts for you to review with your child. Agreement is signed and dated by all parties.

➢ Talking Points Defined—Companion to the Rules of Engagement; provides brief description of the talking points you'll be discussing—giving you the information you need for your discussion.

➢ Cell Phone Only Contract

➢ Social Networking and Internet Only Contract

➢ Warning Notice 1—No Consequences

➢ Warning Notice 2—First Level of Consequences

➢ Warning Notice 3—Second Level of Consequences

➢ Discussion Worksheets for Each Warning Notice

➢ Final Notice—Termination of abused technology for a duration of time selected by you

➢ Reinstatement Notice with Warning—Once final notice has been issued and duration of termination has been completed, technology is reinstated with warning.

➢ The Ignore/Block/Report Program

➢ Facebook Rules to Live By

➢ Consequences of Sexting

➢ The Warning Signs of Textual Harassment

➢ Resources and Support—Local
resources are included in one place

➢ **BONUS:** When the rules are broken,
to be on the same page to enforce the consequences.
We've included the "whys" behind the importance
of standing united when delivering consequences.
This will help parents work together throughout
the punishment process.

A Parent's Legal Responsibility

In the end, parents are legally responsible and liable for
their child's actions when that child is a minor. But, did
you know that parents are liable for their adult-child's
actions if the child is still financially dependent upon
their parents?

Your insurance coverage for these types of exposures
are questionable, depending on specific allegations,
damages, legal liability, and the coverage you have on
your homeowner's policy under the personal liability
section. Contact your insurance broker to make sure you
have the appropriate coverage for your individual needs.

Parent's Guide Fact: Ask your insurance broker if
a personal umbrella will provide you with protection
for and of your child's online actions that might result in a lawsuit.

• •

Throughout the remaining chapters, you will learn about mobile messaging in a teen's world, Facebook fundamentals as they relate to teenagers, what you need to know about social media, and everything about cyberbullies. By the end of this book, you'll realize how important it is to stay connected and involved in your child's online life in order to keep them safe and secure.

2

· ·

Mobile Messaging
and Your Children

In the world of parenting, we can't begin to count the ways we worry about our children! Learning to navigate the world of mobile messaging is becoming more and more difficult as technology advances. Text messaging is a great way to keep the lines of communication open with your busy teenagers, but I'm positive that you've also noticed the not-so-great tendencies, dangers, and bad judgment that also exist with mobile messaging.

With over five billion text messages being exchanged daily, mobile messaging is the Ferrari of the social networking super-highway with texting, BlackBerry messaging, Facebooking, and tweeting leading the way. Now that 285 million Americans are communicating at warp speed, using more mobile devices than ever (smartphones, iPads, eReaders, etc.), it's even more important for you to learn the basics, become tech-savvy, and teach your children to be wise online.

One of the newest silent epidemics in the world of texting is textual harassment, a form of harassment sent by text message with the intent to threaten physical harm, harass, or bully. All across America, parents have growing concerns and are desperate for answers about bullies who deliver malicious and cruel threats by text.

Parent's Guide Tip: When teens are harassed, they keep it to themselves, which is why the vast majority of textual harassment cases go unreported. Children are embarrassed and don't want to tell anyone what's happening to them, and parents are usually the last to know.

How Teens Use Their Phones

The CTIA Wireless survey conducted in December 2009 revealed that 91 percent of Americans are communicating at warp speed by mobile device. It's a fact that 75 percent of America's teens have cell phones and primarily use them to send text messages, update their social networking sites, and take pictures.

According to the 2010 mobile access study completed by Pew Research Center, cell phones are not just used for calling or texting anymore. Phones have become MP3 players, cameras, video recording devices, and pocket-sized social networking devices.

According to Pew's most recent study, teens with smart phones are avid users of their extra features:

➢ 87 percent text message regularly

- ➢ 83 percent use their phones to take pictures
- ➢ 64 percent share pictures with others
- ➢ 60 percent play music on their phones
- ➢ 46 percent play games on their phones
- ➢ 32 percent exchange videos on their phones
- ➢ 31 percent exchange instant messages on their phones
- ➢ 27 percent go online on their phones
- ➢ 21 percent use e-mail on their phones

Parent's Guide Tip: Almost all teenagers who have cell phones use the text message function more than any other function on their cell phone.

Because our children are using their cell phones to text, take pictures, record videos, and access the Internet, possibly all at the same time, it's becoming more difficult to make sure they are making good decisions while they are accessing the power that technology offers.

Teens' Texting Stats

As of December 2009, statistics from a CTIA Wireless study show that teens ages twelve to nineteen have the highest levels of text messaging activity:

- ➢ Teens average more than 3,000 texts a month
- ➢ Teens average 120 phone calls a month
- ➢ Some teens exceed 10,000 texts a month

Teens use their phones to text much more than they use their phones to make calls. In fact, teenagers keep their phones on vibrate and many never check their voicemail. Naturally, there are those teens that exceed the average, sending several thousands of texts a month without ever making a call.

> **Parent's Guide Tip:** A teenager is connected to their cell phone 100 percent of the time.

A recent study released by the American Public Health Association in 2010 suggests that there is an apparent link between excessive messaging, referred to as "hyper-texting" (over 120 text messages a day) and risky behaviors like binge drinking, using drugs, fighting, and promiscuity. The study was conducted at twenty public high schools in the Cleveland area and based on more than 4,200 confidential surveys completed by the high school students of those schools.

The study also revealed that those teens who "hyper-text" are more susceptible to peer pressure and also have permissive or absent parents. "If parents are monitoring their children's texting and social networking, they're probably monitoring other activities as well," said Dr. Scott Frank, the study's lead author. If your child sends over 3,600 text messages a month, I recommend that you take cell phone and social media monitoring seriously to eliminate any potential exposure to risky behaviors.

What Age is the Right Age for a Cell Phone?

What age is the right age? There's no right or wrong answer, because each child and situation is different. *The Parent's Guide* makes the following general age and service recommendations when it comes to allowing your child to have a cell phone:

Ages up to seven—Cell phones are generally not appropriate for children in this age group. Even the most mature seven-year-old isn't ready for the responsibilities of having a cell phone, such as keeping it charged and *not* losing it.

Ages eight to ten—For this age group, consider a cell phone that's designed for children, such as texting phones, and add the unlimited texting plan if necessary. These phones offer much tighter controls than regular phones, are great for younger children because they have smaller keyboards for young children's fingers, and they don't access the Internet. Be sure to add a "parental controls feature" to their wireless number, which will allow you to control when your child can text and limit when they can't. The parental control feature also provides your child with the ability to "block" anyone who harasses or threatens them by call or text. Contact your wireless provider to have the MMS (sending photos and videos by text) feature disabled to avoid the risk of and exposure to sexting. Consider purchasing insurance and the location/zoning service as well.

Ages eleven to thirteen—Choose the cell phone that fits your family's needs, and then add the unlimited texting plan to your child's number. Be sure to add a "parental control" feature to the number, which will allow you to control when your child can text. The parental control feature also provides your child the ability to "block" anyone who harasses or threatens them by text message. With parental controls, you will also be able to restrict Internet access and the ability to purchase items from their phones. Consider purchasing insurance and the location/zoning service for this age group. Contact your wireless provider to have the MMS (sending photos and videos by text) feature disabled to avoid the risk and exposure to sexting.

Ages fourteen to seventeen—Choose a smartphone that your child selects (and fits within your family's budget) and then add the unlimited texting plan. Be sure to add a "parental controls" feature to their number, which will allow you to control when your child can text. The parental control feature also provides your child the ability to block anyone who harasses or threatens them by call or text. With parental controls, you will also be able to limit Internet access and the ability to purchase items from their phones. Consider purchasing insurance and the location/zoning service for this age group. Consider limiting the ability to send pictures and videos by disabling the MMS feature. If you let them keep the MMS feature, monitor photos and videos often, and, if necessary, contact your wireless company to have the MMS feature disabled. Limit the times of day (and night) that the phone can be used, based on the age, maturity level, and past performance of your child.

> **Parent's Guide Tip:** Be sure to obtain your child's cell phone password if they have added one.

Important: Because more than 40 percent of teenagers are now updating their Facebook status by way of their mobile device, you will need to execute the "Rules of Engagement" and review the "Ten Facebook Rules to Live By" with your teenager. Both of these documents can be found in the resource section in the back of this book.

*A **Parent's Guide** Story Submission: "My eight-year-old daughter received a request for a naked photo of herself from her eight-year-old classmate. I had no idea I had to worry about sexting at her young age! I searched the Internet and found the One-Click Safety Kit. I immediately used the 'Rules of Engagement' from the kit to help me discuss the dos and don'ts with my daughter."*

In the case of this father, whose eight-year-old daughter was asked for a sext, he needed to make sure his daughter didn't get herself into text-message trouble by taking the following steps:

- ➤ Have "the talk" about the responsibilities of a cell phone, and explain what sexting is and how it's not OK (yes, even if they are only are eight years old).

- ➤ Execute the "Rules of Engagement" for cell phone usage, which is in the back of this book. For the downloadable and editable version—it's included in the One-Click Safety Kit that can be found online at: www.OneClickSafetyKit.com.

➤ Add a parental control feature to her wireless number and teach *her* how to Ignore/Block/ Report.

➤ Restrict any further calls or texts that are sent from her eight-year-old classmate who asked for the "sext" by blocking his wireless number.

➤ Disable the MMS feature—this will prevent photos and videos from being sent from her phone.

Watch Your Wallet

Unsuspecting parents have gone through the roof after opening that first month's phone bill. *Surprise!* Before parents have had a chance to select a text plan, their teen joined the magical world of texting. They're shocked to discover a $997 bill—all from the 9,786 text messages sent the month before. How could their teen possibly send that many texts within just a few weeks? Remember, teens rely on text messaging as their primary socializing and communication tool. With a teenager, be sure to add the "unlimited texting" option to your wireless plan, avoiding the potential for overage charges.

Parent's Guide Tip: It's not uncommon for teenagers to send over 10,000 text messages a month.

Parental Controls = Peace of Mind

Because most mobile phones include many bells and whistles, you'll need to take special precautions by adding parental control services to your teen's wireless number.

For a small monthly fee (usually five dollars a month), all major wireless providers in the United States offer a parental control feature, allowing parents to "set text boundaries" and help with:

➢ Limiting the number of texts sent/received

➢ Restricting the times of day the cell phone can be used

➢ GPS location and zoning (this is sometimes a separate service)

➢ Restricting online purchases

➢ Controlling what number can be blocked from calling or sending/receiving text messages

➢ Filtering content/blocking Internet usage

Text message content monitoring is not usually offered within parental control services due to confidentiality issues. If you feel you need to monitor the content of your child's text messages, you'll need to purchase special software that has text-monitoring capabilities. I recommend that you Google "Parental Control Software for Mobile Phones" to locate software that monitors text content. If you're going to monitor content, you *must* tell your child what you are doing and why.

> **Parent's Guide Tip:** If you have reason to distrust your child's texting activity, consider disabling their ability to text instead of just monitoring content.

Child Locator Services

The ability to locate a lost child is priceless. Almost all wireless providers offer the ability to add GPS tracking and zoning as an additional service for a monthly fee. One of the benefits of this service is that it allows you to locate a family member's cell phone from your computer or phone at any time, with no distance limitations (within the United States). Notifications of boundary violations that you have set for your child can also be set to notify you automatically by text message if your child is somewhere they shouldn't be. Additionally, this service allows you to pinpoint exactly where a cell phone is, as long as the cell phone is on.

Adding a GPS locator service may not only help keep track of your children all of the time, but it can definitely save lives. Location detection services provide an incredible tracking tool should your teen ever run away or be kidnapped.

Practice Safe Text

These days, practicing safe text is just as important as practicing safe sex. It's up to parents to teach their children about how to practice safe texting, and what never to do. Remind them that:

➤ Everything sent by text message is not private, like most children think.

➤ When a message is sent by text, it can be instantly forwarded to anyone within seconds.

➤ Conversations by text message can be used as evidence by the police.

➤ A text message can end up being posted on Facebook, Twitter, or any other social media site. The same thing goes for photos and videos sent by text message. Children should assume that nothing sent by text remains private.

Parent's Guide Tip: Teens should always practice safe text with every message they send to avoid a private message from becoming public.

Sex + Texting = Sexting

Sexting: A "sext" is defined as a sexual text message or sexually explicit photo that is delivered by text message (often called mobile messaging) using SMS and/or MMS technology.

Sexting is a terrifying concept for any parent and has become more and more prevalent within the teen community. Sexting involves the sending of inappropriate and/or sexually explicit photos or videos of themselves or inappropriate messages that are texted to boyfriends, girlfriends, and even strangers.

Thirty-nine percent of teens have admitted to sexting and 51 percent of teen girls feel pressured to send explicit photos, with the numbers increasing at an alarming rate. "Not my child" is what parents want to believe. But the statistics show there are many teens participating in this racy and growing trend of sexting.

Take sexting one step further to the brink of total destruction when you realize that the recipient of a sext has the ability to easily forward and share these inappropriate photos or messages with anyone he or she chooses. Who knows where these pictures could end up? The possibilities are frighteningly endless.

The second a child hits the "send" button or uploads a photo to the Internet that includes a "sext," serious consequences that can result are:

➤ Potential to be arrested and charged for child pornography

➤ Requirement to register as a sex offender

➤ Humiliation among peers because a once-private photo was posted online and/or forwarded to others

➤ Injuries, suicides, and attacks can be the end result

➤ Attraction of stalkers/online predators

➤ Hazing/name-calling

➤ Sexual harassment, textual harassment, or sextortion

➤ Possible expulsion from school

Sexting is practiced more often than you think. Teens (and adults) have been arrested for sending explicit photos of children by text or for posting them online. Make it a habit to monitor photos on your child's cell phone, mobile device, and social media sites such as Facebook, MySpace, or any other social media outlet to which your teen belongs.

Parent's Guide Tip: 40 percent of teenage girls said they have sent sexually suggestive messages or photos as a "joke."

No parent wants their teen to be arrested for sexting, which is illegal when the exchange of a naked photo occurs between minors. Beyond that, sexting carries the risk of:

➢ **Teen Suicide**— Results from private, inappropriate photos, videos, or messages that become public, causing humiliation and devastation

➢ **Textual Harassment**—When texts are sent to harass, bully, embarrass, threaten, or destroy another person

➢ **Sextortion**—When a person uses guilt, power, or knowledge of a certain secret to force another person into providing sexually explicit photos, having sex, or performing sexual favors

➢ **Peer Pressure**—Feeling pressured to text or post something you don't want to

➢ **Inappropriate Message**—Meant for only the recipient but can get sent to friends, teachers, coaches, parents, and even strangers

➢ **Breakups/Relationship Problems**—Forced to stay in a relationship for fear of inappropriate photos surfacing somewhere unexpected

➢ **Textual-Sexual Harassment**—An aggressive, sexually motivated message sent to a person over whom the aggressor has some power

Sexting is an unfortunate reality that we need to face and work to prevent our children from participating in. To do this, we will need to have the "sit down" with our children to set text boundaries and explain the potentially serious consequences of *any* kind of sexting.

When you sit down with your child to have "the talk" about the birds and the bees and the dangers of drinking and driving, you will need to include the dangers of sexting in your conversation. Children need to understand how they could be exploiting themselves or others if they decide to participate in any kind of sexting activities. (Sexting is addressed in the "Rules of Engagement" contract in the back of this book.)

Once a child has attached an inappropriate picture or video to a text and sent it, they can never take it back. It's important to explain to your child that the "BFF" today could be the "enemy" of tomorrow who might decide to forward that very private photo to all of his friends. Make sure your child understands the serious consequences that arise from sexting and how it can negatively change their lives forever!

Be sure to take proactive steps to help prevent sexting by opening the lines of communication with your child about sexting and regularly monitoring their texts and cell phone pictures and videos. Be sure you have reviewed and executed the "Rules of Engagement" contract found in the back of this book and online at www.OneClick-SafetyKit.com. If you follow this process, you'll be ten steps ahead of the sexting epidemic that's taking a toll on our teenagers all across the country.

Sexting Prevention

A quick and easy way to prevent your teen from sexting is to request your service provider to restrict the sending of pictures and videos from their cell phone. Most wireless providers don't charge to eliminate this service, and your teens will still be able to text. They can still take photos, but they won't be able to share them with their friends.

There are software applications you can purchase to monitor all of your teen's cell phone and Internet activity, including photos and text message content. Some of these software applications will also allow you to print a detailed report with all the information included. If you leave the monitoring of text messages and photos to a software program, there will be no guarantee that all potential damaging content will be recognized.

Children can outsmart even the smartest of software. Most children whose parents monitor using software use newer technologies (available in the iTunes App store) to dodge and "work around" any type of monitoring software. The fact is that you will probably never know that your child is using technology to avoid your monitoring. Remember, there's *no* substitute for your "personal" parenting.

It's also necessary to monitor any camera, video recorder, or webcam as inappropriate photos and videos can be easily uploaded to any social networking site, such as Facebook or YouTube, from these devices.

Many parents don't feel that they have the right to monitor their child's private conversations, photos, or videos, but you do. What's important to remember is that you are most likely paying your child's monthly cell phone bill and providing access to the Internet. You are the parent, which makes you the authority in your household. It's your primary responsibility to do whatever you need to do in order to protect your children and avoid a one-click nightmare from occurring in your home.

Parent's Guide Tip: Execute the "Rules of Engagement" for cell phone and Internet use, found in the back of this book.

Textual Harassment

One of the newest silent epidemics in the world of mobile messaging is textual harassment, a form of harassment sent by text message with the intent to threaten physical harm, harass, or bully. Across America, parents have growing concerns and are desperate for answers on how to protect their children from bullies who deliver malicious and cruel threats by text. Why has the popularity of textual harassment grown at such an alarming rate?

➤ Instant and Accessible—75 percent of US children between the ages of twelve and seventeen have a cell phone.

➤ Hide Behind Technology—two out of three teen texters say they are more likely to use their cell phones to send a message versus face-to-face confrontation.

➤ One in four teens admit they have been called names, harassed, or have put someone down by text message.

➤ Most parents are unaware their child is being harassed.

When children are harassed, the vast majority of them keep it to themselves, which is why most teen-related textual harassment cases go unreported or even undetected. As a result of the hundreds of personal interviews and discussions I've had with teens, it became evident that teens are embarrassed when they get harassed and don't want to tell anyone what's happening to them. They won't confide in their best friends, and they will rarely tell their parents.

Unfortunately, parents and teachers are the last to know, often finding out that their child is being harassed by text after the damage has been done. It's up to parents to educate their children and talk openly about how to deal with text bantering bullies before an occurrence happens—not after. Your conversation needs to happen much like it would when you speak about drinking, sex, or drugs.

> **Parent's Guide Tip:** When children are harassed by social media and text messages, it's common that they won't confide in anyone.

Watch For the Warning Signs

Harassment delivered by text or online is about the bully who can reach out to their target at any time and place.

- ➢ 43 percent of teens admit to being harassed, bullied, or threatened online or by text.
- ➢ The majority of those teens that are harassed by text message are female.
- ➢ One in five teenagers experiences online harassment on a regular basis.

Today's headlines are full of children being virtually attacked by text message. They're being cyberbullied, threatened, and harassed on a daily basis, falling victim to the perils of the easy exchange of information that all mobile devices offer. Most parents are aware of the text harassment problem, but their first thought is to immediately dismiss the threat because it sounds impossible that their child could be involved.

We hear about tragic situations that have occurred as a result of text harassment on the news, on the radio, from our friends, and everywhere else. Children are getting beaten up both physically and emotionally, with some even dying as a result. We just don't want to believe that textual harassment could happen to our children, under our watch, in our home. Believe me when I tell you that your teen knows someone right now who has been or is currently being bullied or threatened by text message.

A major hurdle for parents is detecting the early warning signs of textual harassment. With most teens having their own cell phones, how can parents know when texting gets to the point of harassment? Yes, there are signs, but they are subtle and often silent:

➢ Self-isolation—even from their best friends

➢ Extreme emotional and irrational behavior

➢ Sudden loss of their favorite interests

➢ Sudden reduction of social activities

➢ Strange behavior including texting at all hours of the night

➢ Continuous sleep deprivation

➢ Extreme possessiveness of their phone

➢ Extreme secrecy about whom they're texting

Because many of the signs of textual harassment seem to be "common" for teens, you will need to pay close attention to your child (especially between the ages of thirteen and sixteen) and look for extreme cases that go beyond your teen's typical "adolescent" behaviors.

Review Cell Phone Applications, Photos, and Phone Bills

Constantly check your child's cell phone for inappropriate applications, photos, or text messages. Review your child's cell phone bill for unrecognizable numbers and ask your child to whom they belong. If they refuse to tell you, then call the number yourself. Numbers called are date- and time-stamped on your bill. If a number that you don't recognize appears on your statement at late hours for long periods of time, or numerous text messages appear from a number that you don't know, it's cause for suspicion.

> **Parent's Guide Tip:** You have every right to monitor your child's cell phone, especially since you're the one most likely paying the bill.

Learn to Ignore/Block/Report

The Ignore/Block/Report Program was developed as the direct result of my teenage daughter being harassed and bullied on her cell phone. When you teach your children the power of "blocking" their frenemy's cell phone number, you have empowered your child to instantly defuse a bad situation. Talk to your child about the power of being in control, and teach them the simple I/B/R three-step process:

1. IGNORE—Don't respond (and make a copy of the message if you feel it's necessary).

2. BLOCK—Call your wireless provider or go online to have the number blocked.

3. REPORT—Report the harassment to parents and the police when necessary.

Textual harassment is an unfortunate reality that has developed as a result of the growth and popularity of texting. It has grown to such a degree that special laws have been put in place to contain the problem. As these laws will vary from state to state, you should check to see if the state where you live has such a law. In many states, a single unsolicited text message that threatens physical harm or is obscene is enough to meet the definition of textual harassment.

The I/B/R Program will help both you and your children neutralize and defend themselves against bullies who harass, threaten, or bully by text or online.

> **Parent's Guide Tip**: To get your free downloadable version of the Ignore/Block/Report Program, visit www.OneClickSafteyKit.com

For more information about the different state laws that govern electronic harassment, cyberstalking, and cyberbullying, visit the National Conference of State Legislatures: www.ncsl.org/IssuesResearch/TelecommunicationsInformationTechnology.

Teen Emergencies

If your child is ever caught in an emergency situation, text messaging is the technology you want them to have immediate access to. The technology associated with mobile messaging offers benefits that phone calls can't, such as:

➢ Your teens might not be near a landline, but you can be sure they'll *never* be without their cell phones.

➢ A text can be executed silently and instantly, which allows a text to be sent when silence is critical to safety.

➢ Texts require less battery power than a wireless call, so if the phone's battery is too low to make a call or landlines are down, and/or there's a low wireless signal, a text can still be sent.

Text messages can be sent to multiple family members at the same time, instantly letting everyone know where they are, if they're in trouble, and what their present situation is. Having the ability to respond instantly to an urgent request for help is critical to both the sender and the receiver.

Mobile Communication Offers Additional Student Support

In November of 2009, Pottsgrove High School, located in Pottstown, Pennsylvania, experienced the tragic deaths of two students in an automobile accident. The social and emotional impact of these sudden deaths and subsequent conversations with students led the administration to seek novel ways to offer support to students and their friends who are experiencing barriers to learning, such as drugs, alcohol, or mental health issues.

The Pottsgrove High School principal, Christopher L. Shaffer, had seen a video showcasing a preventative tool employed by stadiums that encouraged fans to text into a central command for assistance with crowd control or unruly behavior. In light of recent events, he began to think of this tool's potential application in education, specifically in addressing the needs of his school. The company (www.guestassist.net) delivers mobile-phone-based communications that allow an enterprise, such as a school, to interact with their students. The cost for this service can be as low as two dollars a student. The cost for Pottsgrove runs about $2,000 annually.

While cell phone use in class is against their school policy, a "technology zone" was established in the Pottsgrove cafeteria where students were permitted to use their phones during lunch. With the implementation of this system, a cutting-edge technology commonly utilized on college campuses, students have communicated via text to the operators (school administration and a few select teachers) about bullying, various concerns about their friends, and knowledge of drug use. Signs and video news bulletins have been circulating throughout this particular high school with the following message:

CONCERNED?
Text "Falcons"and your concern to 12468.

Students are encouraged to text concerns related to bullying, possible drug and alcohol abuse, self-injury, and other topics that may hinder student learning. All text messages are filtered into a website that is constantly monitored by trained teachers and administrators. Students receive a message in return thanking them for their concern, asking for more specific details, or in cases deemed urgent, asking them to report to an administrator or counselor for support. Incoming information is then passed on to the school personnel who can best provide assistance to the student.

In the first month of operation, the Falcon Assist program had provided support to at least a dozen students. It's great that students care and show concern for their peers!

The school is now asking for parents to help provide support to their students by utilizing the text messaging service, saying, "If you feel your son/daughter or their friends are in need of assistance then please text "Falcons" and your concern to 12468."

This system is simple yet powerful, as it allows for anonymous communication, has a web-based control system for easy access, and has the ability to tag conversations for future reports based on the type of concern or issue.

Campus Alerts

A nineteen-year-old sophomore at the University of Texas opened fire in September of 2010 while running through the Austin campus with an AK-47, eventually killing himself. The good news is that no one else was hurt. Most of the credit for the absence of fatalities goes to the university's crisis-management program.

As part of the school's emergency alert system and protocol, their text messaging system reached out to more than 43,000 people, warning students, faculty, and staff to stay away from the area where the gunman was located. The text message also advised students on campus to remain indoors and wait for further instructions.

I *highly* recommend that you review your school's crisis-management plan to verify what would happen if a situation like this occurred at your school. Many educational institutions have already implemented a text messaging system that warns students, parents, faculty, and staff in the event of an emergency. Consider the following questions:

➢ Does your child's elementary, middle, high school, or university have an emergency text messaging system in place? A service such as Mobile Campus provides real-time emergency alerts for schools across the country.

➢ Are you and your family members listed on the emergency text recipient list?

> ➤ If your child's school has yet to implement an emergency text messaging system, when is it planned to be added?

> ➤ If there is an emergency, who will be notified and how?

> ➤ Does your school have an internet based "bulletin board" where parents can go for up-to-date information, including during an emergency (this could be a Facebook page)?

What makes campus alerts by text message so efficient? The majority of Americans own cell phones and carry them with them almost all of the time. During an emergency situation, an instant text notification would be sent directly to your cell phone, which is better than a message left on your home voicemail that you probably wouldn't receive for hours.

Distracted Driving Kills

In case of an emergency, having a cell phone in your teenager's car while they are on the road is a prudent decision to make, but distracted driving kills more than 6,000 people a year and injures another 500,000. According to the Pew Research Center who surveyed teens about texting and driving:

> ➤ 34 percent of teenagers between the ages of sixteen and seventeen admit to texting while driving.

> ➤ According to the Insurance Institute of Highway Safety, those who text while driving increase their risk of an accident by 50 percent.

- ➢ 50 percent of Americans ages twelve to seventeen say they've been in the car with someone who has texted while behind the wheel.

- ➢ 80 percent of teenage girls and 58 percent of teenage boys admit to texting behind the wheel.

- ➢ Drivers who talk or text while driving have much slower response times than those who don't. According to the University of Utah, they have slower reaction times than drivers whose blood-alcohol levels are at 0.08.

A recent public service campaign by AT&T focused on the last text message that was sent or received before a fatal accident occurred as a result of texting while driving. In one of the accidents, a mother noted the last text her daughter received was "where u at?" . . . Her daughter had read the text while driving into oncoming traffic, resulting in the loss of her life.

The Parent's Guide wants all drivers to declare their car a "No Phone Zone" and join our cause. Be sure to talk to your children about the repercussions of texting while driving, and have them take the "No Phone Zone Pledge" at www.ShawnEdgington.com.

Text Addiction

Your teens probably have a difficult time being "in the moment" with people because of the constant stream of text messages they are receiving. It can be difficult to gain their full attention when their eyes are constantly looking down at their cell phones to read their messages. It's impossible for them to be 100 percent present in a face-to-face conversation, focus on homework, or hang out with family when your teen's primary concern is text messages.

It's a parent's job to set priorities and enforce text boundaries. Establish how much texting is too much and make sure your teen's texting doesn't become an addiction. To take the easy way out of micro-managing your child's cell phone usage: Add a parental control feature to your child's wireless number, and then set the days and times that they can text and/or talk (or the times that they can't).

> **Parent's Guide Tip:** Children often stay up until two in the morning text messaging. Use a parental controls feature to turn off the ability to text at specific times, set by you.

• •

You've learned throughout this chapter the many ways you can take charge and create text balance, how to defend against textual harassment, and the benefits and dangers of using mobile messaging. If you're finding managing your child's texting habits an impossible task to do on your own, add a parental controls feature to their wireless number (about five dollars a month for most providers). It eliminates the constant micro-managing you most likely have to do when it comes to their usage and provides additional benefits like empowering your child to instantly block a number from someone who's harassing them by text message.

You've also learned how important it is to communicate, to stay tuned-in to what your children are doing, and to monitor all mobile devices for inappropriate content.

If you're looking for more tools that you can use to help keep your children safe and secure online visit www.OneClickSafetyKit.com. You'll find free downloadable resources and other information that will help prevent a one-click nightmare from occurring in your home.

3

· ·

Social Media:
What Parents Need to Know

Think of social media as a group of Internet-based applications that allow for the creation and exchange of user-generated content. In short, it's the blending of technology and social interaction that delivers endless online possibilities.

Social media comes in a variety of forms, including Internet forums, web logs ("blogs"), social micro-blogging, wikis, podcasts, pictures, video, and social bookmarking. In general, there are six different types of social media: collaborative projects, blogs and micro-blogs, content communities, social networking sites, virtual game worlds, and virtual communities.

➢ In the United States, social networking now accounts for 22 percent of all time spent online.

➢ Twitter processed more than one billion tweets in December 2009 and averages almost forty million tweets per day.

➢ Over 25 percent of US Internet page views occurred at one of the top social networking sites during the month of December 2009—up from 13.8 percent a year before.

Teens use social media to stay in touch with their friends within a social networking community and for playing online games, and in most cases, it's risk-free and good fun. But, there are dangers that we need to keep a watchful eye on, such as online predators, cyberbullies, online harassment, and the locating of adult websites.

Teens and Social Networks

According to a survey from a sampling of US teens between thirteen and seventeen years old completed in April of 2010 by Roiworld, teens typically spend two hours a day on the Internet.

On average, 80 percent of that time is spent on a social network—and you guessed it, Facebook is the social network of choice. Are you wondering if Facebook is the new MySpace? Absolutely! With fifty million teenagers (and growing) between the ages of thirteen and seventeen actively accessing their Facebook profile versus MySpace's sixteen million active users (and declining), Facebook is by far the number-one social network preferred by teenagers.

In addition, Roiworlds' survey found that:

➤ 90 percent of teens have a profile on a social networking site.

➤ 73 percent of teens play games on social networking sites.

- ➢ 69 percent of teens have a Facebook account.
- ➢ 64 percent of teens have a profile on YouTube.
- ➢ 41 percent of teens have a profile on MySpace.
- ➢ 43 percent of teens spend money on social networking sites (usually playing games).
- ➢ 49 percent of teens reported that they have an allowance to spend money online.

Teens love to update their Facebook statuses often, using their mobile devices when they're not next to their computers. Teens are also great multi-taskers . . . they can update their social networking sites while they're doing homework, texting, watching videos, and listening to music.

How Teens Network Online

Of the social networking sites, Facebook—which hit five hundred million users in 2010—ran away with first prize for the most users in all age groups. Nearly 85 percent of all time spent in the social media sector was spent on Facebook, compared to just 5.6 percent for MySpace, the runner-up. Twitter and Blogger tied for third place with 1.1 percent. By the end of 2011, I expect YouTube to make it into one of the top three spots.

The time that teens spend online has dramatically increased over the last twelve months, especially within the social media sector. According to surveys conducted by Roiworld, when teenagers network online, they:

- Post photos and videos from their mobile devices
- Build online profiles and communities
- Connect with friends
- Send photos to friends
- Play games
- Watch videos
- Broadcast what they're doing to everyone in their network
- "Check In" by mobile phone—letting everyone know their location by using GPS technology

What has become more evident with the increased time dedicated to a teen's favorite online game, network, or video is the elevated risk associated with their behaviors, such as:

- The online world can feel anonymous, so rules are often broken
- Ability to post inappropriate content
- Addiction to their favorite online activity
- Teens can feel they're not accountable for their actions
- Inappropriate behavior—teens with bad intentions such as a cyberbully
- Finding pornographic sites, violent sites, or hate group sites

You can reduce these risks by counseling your child about the way they communicate online, limiting their time online, monitoring their social media sites, and by executing the "Rules of Engagement" contract. If the rules are broken, follow through with the consequences that are spelled out in the contract in order to keep the boundaries strong and solid. Children need to know that we, as parents, will enforce the boundaries that have been set in place. Finally, it's *so* important to continuously reinforce the need to protect their image when communicating within a social network.

Maturity is Required

Maturity is something that's unique to every child. Many young teens lack the ability to make good decisions on a consistent basis. Facebook requires children to be at least thirteen years old to open an account, but that doesn't mean that on their thirteenth birthday you are required to let them get an account. You'll need to be the judge of when your child is mature enough to handle the responsibility that goes with using any social networking sites, no matter what their age is.

Prior to giving them the green light, review and discuss the twenty talking points in the "Rules of Engagement—Social Media Contract" available at www.one-clicksafetykit.com. If you decide you want to add some of your own rules to the agreement, you can customize the contract by making any additions that are important to your family.

Example: You must maintain a 3.0 GPA to keep your technology privileges.

Upon reviewing this contract with your child, you will become more aware of their maturity level by how they respond and communicate with you. You will know right away if they are ready to handle the responsibility that comes with using today's technology. You may decide that you need to hold off and revisit the issue at a later time.

How to Protect Your Teen's Online Image

As a parent, protecting your teenager's online image is one of the most important (and difficult) jobs you have. Remember all of the crazy things you did as a teen without giving a thought about what you were doing? Thank goodness our every move wasn't documented on the Internet for everyone to see like it is today, with cameras and videos on every cell phone recording every moment. Unfortunately, most of our children's missteps can be easily splashed across the Internet by their friends or by their own naivety and lack of maturity. They'll need to learn that anything posted on the Internet will remain there for everyone to see.

Be sure your child knows how important it is to think twice before posting, because any pictures, videos, language, or comments that end up online will most likely be visible to an entire host of individuals, including: other parents, potential employers, educators, coaches, teachers, and even the police. Your child will also need to understand how important it is to control what content their friends post about them—an extremely difficult thing to manage. Most older and more experienced teens who are aware of the importance of protecting their online image will delete their "offending friends" who post inappropriate content.

To help with online image protection, daily monitoring is a great idea, especially for teens between the ages of twelve and sixteen. This age group tends to get a little "out of control" with what they talk about and post online. These tips will help you protect your teen's online image:

➢ Remind your children that once they post information online, they can't get it back.

➢ Set all privacy settings to restrict who can see and access their site.

➢ Monitor all of your teen's social networking sites. Watch what information they're posting and read their comments.

➢ Set a Google Alert for each of your children's names and schools. (It's important to know when your child's school hits the news.)

➢ Review your child's "friends" list often. Don't accept a list of friends that is too long—it usually means they're "friending" people they don't know.

➢ Limit your children's online "friends" to people they actually know.

➢ Watch for information that should stay private. Social Security numbers, street addresses, phone numbers, or family financial information like bank accounts and credit card numbers are all private information and should never be posted online.

➤ Encourage children to trust their gut—if they have suspicions regarding unsolicited requests from strangers, teach them about the Ignore/Block/Report system.

➤ Encourage your teens to tell you if they feel uncomfortable or threatened as a result of something happening online. Make sure they block the offender.

➤ Talk to your teens about inappropriate sex talk and let them know that it will not be tolerated.

➤ Talk to your teens about the importance of not standing by and watching others get harassed or bullied online.

➤ If your teen gets bullied online, have them report concerns to you. Be sure to make copies of all material information, and report the incident to the social networking site. If necessary, contact the police.

➤ Watch for inappropriate groups or pages that have been connected to your child's site, such as hate groups.

➤ Tell your child that impersonating someone else or stealing someone else's identity is absolutely unacceptable. (This is accomplished by stealing/using someone else's username and password.) Immediately disable their social media accounts if you find evidence of this.

Unfortunately, it's not uncommon for online predators to set up false profiles, use a fake picture and a cool name to attract young teenagers to their networking site so they can take advantage of them. If a predator of any kind targets your child, teach them to *not* respond, block the offender and immediately report them to the hosting site. You will also need to report the offender to the police. If you don't, they may never get caught.

It's crucial that you help your teen protect their social media profile. If a profile is ever created for your child without their knowledge or if their profile is altered without their permission, contact the company that runs the site to have it taken down immediately. This is critical, as it usually means your child is being targeted by a cyberbully.

> **Parent's Guide Tip:** Rewards are a great way to incent your child for good online behavior.

Monitoring Behavior

One of the ways to keep a more watchful eye on your child's online behavior is to use social media monitoring tools. When you are using monitoring software, the company will notify you about all of your child's social profiles across the web (you will need to know which e-mail address or username they have used to set up each site). You'll get activity reports and alerts for inappropriate content, and it will help you stay on top of changes made to any of their sites.

SafetyWeb is an online service geared toward parents who wish to keep tabs on what their children are doing online. SafetyWeb checks across forty-five different social networking sites to see if your child has a registered public profile and it monitors those accounts for any potentially threatening activities. Monitored platforms include Facebook, Flickr, MySpace, Twitter, and YouTube. It also recognizes LiveJournal as a social network and will monitor that site as well.

The service will notify you if your child has posted anything potentially unsafe or inappropriate, checking categories for words related to drugs and alcohol, sex, depression, profanity, and cyberbullying.

McGruff software takes online monitoring a step further: It records every move your child makes on the Internet, covering everything from instant message logs to search terms used on Google. Parents can keep a close eye on their children and discuss any behavior found to be dangerous or inappropriate.

Whether or not you use a software monitoring tool, experts agree that having regular conversations with your children about their online usage is the most important element to keeping them safe and aware of the dangers that exist online. In addition, monitoring software does NOT have the ability to protect your teens online image, nor is it 100 percent accurate.

> **Parent's Guide Tip:** Don't rely 100 percent on monitoring software—it's not a substitute for parenting.

The Potpourri of Online Scum

A drug ring consisting of older teen boys was successful for years at infiltrating local high schools to sell students marijuana and Ecstasy by posting announcements on a popular social networking site. It turned out that these young men had set up a username under a false identity and spread the word that if anyone wanted to buy drugs, all they had to do was "friend" them, then post their order in "drug code." Special codes were devised so parents and the authorities that were monitoring their social media sites wouldn't know what was being referenced.

It's situations like this that give parents nightmares. However, the access to buying pills, marijuana, etc. has never been easier, thanks to the help of social media. It's extremely easy to purchase prescription drugs online—which is where many of the "drugs of choice" originate. Dealers mix pharmaceutical drugs and then blend them to make pills like Ecstasy—one of the new "drugs of choice"—and it is killing children everywhere.

You may have heard about the serial sex offender who admitted to using Facebook to lure, rape, and murder a seventeen-year-old girl. This particular online predator, a thirty-three-year-old man, fooled his female target into thinking he was a seventeen-year-old teen. This man's fake Facebook profile, with the name of "DJ Pete," had attracted interest from 14,600 visitors, and almost three thousand of them became online "friends." All of these "friends" were females who ranged from the ages of thirteen to thirty-one years old. Once they became friends, DJ Pete would attempt to redirect them to private chat rooms where he would invite them to provide sexually explicit details.

Despite Facebook's attempts to safeguard its users from sexual predators, tens of thousands of registered sex offenders have been able to slip through the cracks.

Another story that made the news was about a Wisconsin teen who was convicted of using Facebook to entrap and blackmail dozens of classmates into having sex with him.

What I'm referring to is the potpourri of online scum. They're everywhere, especially online. Why is this? Because it's so easy (and free) to set up false identities to reach lots of children with little effort. Online scum love to use social networking sites to lure their prey into their sick and disgusting world. How? Our children let their guards down and accept them as "friends." Social networking sites are the perfect place for these online scumsters to hide—another very important reason why it's critical to show your children how to protect themselves online and what signs to watch for, and for you to monitor your teen's social networking sites on a regular basis.

> One in five children are approached by an online predator through social networking sites like MySpace or Facebook.

> ➤ Predators use networking sites to produce and distribute child pornography.

> ➤ Predators encourage the exchange of photos and entice children to meet for sexual and other reasons.

> ➤ Most victims are between the ages of twelve and fifteen.

> ➤ Most victims have not set up privacy and security settings.

> ➤ Most victims willingly engage in conversations with strangers.

> ➤ Most victims tend to be loners with few offline friends.

> ➤ Many children believe they're in contact with someone their own age, not an adult.

> ➤ Most victims are very secret about their Internet activities and have little interest outside of their online world.

> ➤ Online monsters offer gifts or promises to gain acceptance so they can lure their targets into meeting them in person.

What can you do? Be sure to communicate often, teach your kids to only trust people they know, review their online friends regularly, watch for posts and updates that don't add up, and don't allow webcams of any type in your teen's bedroom. Webcams have the ability to transmit high quality and continuous video footage, which can be instantly streamed around the globe via social media sites. When it comes to young teens, webcams are an open invitation for sexual predators, so educate your children and keep a watchful eye on them if your teen has a webcam built into his or her computer.

> **Parent's Guide Tip:** The only way you're going to find out about online predators before it's too late is to personally monitor your child's social networks.

Warn your children that bad people are on the Internet pretending to be someone they are not, and that sending anything that is sexually explicit will most likely end up in the wrong hands. Make sure they understand how important it is to *never* allow anyone to access their social media sites unless they are personal friends.

Rules Will Be Broken

I'm sure you remember the old saying "rules were meant to be broken," and I'm also sure you broke rules when you were a teenager. When it comes to learning the rules of online behavior, you can count on the fact that our teens will learn the same way we did, by making mistakes with what they post online—a difficult way to learn. Expect your rules to be broken—just hope that the breach is minor and repairable, which in most cases it will be.

Expect someone's feelings to be hurt, drama to swirl around the situation, and friendships to be broken. Learning a lesson by making a mistake can be a painful one, but it's still a good way to learn. Unfortunately, because of the permanent nature of the Internet, it's usually much more painful to make mistakes online.

The Importance of Consequences

Parents around the world have testified that restricting cell phone services such as texting and Internet access works well as a consequence for inappropriate use.

One of the most difficult and unpleasant jobs a parent has is enforcing the rules that have been set. You can expect that there will be tension between you and your teenager when rules are being enforced. They may become frustrated, irritated, agitated, depressed, pouty, or downright angry. It can also be a source of displeasure for siblings if they're dragged into the situation.

Typically parents don't take the phone away, as they still need to have the ability to contact their child. A great tool for limiting the bells and whistles that come with almost every cell phone is the parental control feature that is available from your wireless provider for a low monthly fee.

If parents are separated or divorced, or your teen lives in a blended family situation, it's critical that all parents are on the same page. You can expect that discipline will be challenged by your teenager, but don't let this happen. By signing a contract like the "Rules of Engagement" found in the back of this book, parents eliminate any misunderstanding of the consequences to breaking the rules.

The most important, and probably the most difficult, job will be a parent's need to enforce the rules of the contract. If you back off on any of the rules that you've all agreed to, you put both you and your children at risk.

As parents, we all know that discipline is as essential in a healthy family home as it is at work, in the community, and in the military. At home, discipline ensures compliance with the rules set in place. It not only creates healthy boundaries, it also sets the example for your teenager's future as they head out into the workforce.

Although they are not really children anymore, teens lack the maturity to always make the best decisions on their own. Firm boundaries, guidance, and consistency from parents are what teenagers require to become successful adults. The ironic thing about setting boundaries and staying consistent with your teens is that they *really* want you to set boundaries, and they want you to be consistent. Deep down, it's what they expect from their parents.

Parent's Guide Tip: Post a copy of the executed "Rules of Engagement" next to every computer in your home.

Discipline Defined

Disciplinary action programs are common in the workplace. They are used in all industries and in companies of all sizes. A disciplinary action program is a management tool designed to correct and prevent recurrences of improper behavior. One's behavior is considered improper when it violates a stated or universally accepted rule of conduct. There are two things disciplinary actions are *not*:

1. They are *not* a substitute for good, sound parenting.
2. They are *not* a weapon for personal revenge.

Disciplinary action has two goals: correction and prevention. Correction in that the teenager violating the rule will be made abundantly aware of his/her error; and prevention in that the teenager will reach a point where, in the process, the consequences far outweigh the benefits of the action so he/she will not continue the behavior. As a side benefit, siblings will profit from the example and better understand what is accepted as right and wrong.

Your teenager must be given an opportunity to improve. Continued violations should result in increasingly severe disciplinary action and a point will be reached where your teen will either realize the necessity to do the right thing or will assume a defensive, negative attitude, which could lead to the need for counseling.

Rules

As a parent you'll notice that *most* teenagers follow the rules as long as they are clearly stated. Writing them down in the form of a contract and reviewing the contract with your teenager on a regular basis to ensure he/she understands the expectations and the consequences for violating the rules is an excellent method, and it is one that they will encounter later during college and on the job.

Effective rules must be stated in a language that's easy for the teenagers to understand. They should be short, simple, and to the point, which is what you will find with the contracts, warning notices, and information included in the One-Click Safety Kit. An effective disciplinary program should offer teenagers full and complete knowledge of what is expected of them. Rules must be communicated both verbally and in writing and discussed or referred to frequently.

A firm, fair approach must be initiated and maintained with respect to enforcement of the rules. Teenagers are likely to test their boundaries, so parents need to be consistent in maintaining discipline. *Instituting rules and then allowing infractions to occur unchallenged will nullify any effectiveness the rules may have.*

Firmness implies taking actions when necessary. It's very easy for a parent to turn his or her head and give their teenager a break, but this attitude invariably leads to disregard for the rules since the parents did not enforce them. Time and time again, parents send mixed messages because they don't enforce the rules. If your teenager does something wrong and it's not corrected, that teenager has every justification to assume that you'll do nothing the next time the rules are broken. Therefore, you must enforce the consequences when your teen breaks the rules; teens need to get used to the "no exceptions" facts of adult life.

A complete system to help you set boundaries and stick by the consequences has been laid out for you in the One-Click Safety Kit. If you need to customize the system for your family, you can easily make the changes. Whatever you do, stick to the consequences you have outlined with your teen if boundaries are broken. Remember, your sole goal is to keep your children safe and secure at all times.

A Word about Consistency

Although consistency is implied in the previous section, it's worth highlighting because it's the essential element in the process that will make "The Rules of Engagement" successful; a lack of consistency can render the Rules totally useless. Being consistent in the disciplinary action process must take place on two levels:

1. **Between the Parents:** All parents within the household must agree on and be actively involved in the disciplinary process. They must give each infraction the same amount of weight and assert the same consequences. There should be no difference if it's Mom or Dad who addresses a particular offense.

Too often one parent is more lenient than the other. This inconsistency can lead to arguments between parents, which is counterproductive. The goal is to correct and prevent further undesirable behavior on the part of your teenager. If your teenager is aware of this inconsistency (and believe me, they know which parent is the "softie"), he/she will most likely exploit it to his/her own advantage.

Most often it plays out something like the following example: A teen gets caught texting inappropriate messages to someone. The parent who identified the issue says that the teen will lose texting privileges for one week. The teen goes to the other parent in tears or some other heightened emotional state suitable to gaining the sympathy of the other parent and cries that the punishment is too severe. The second parent confronts the first parent, an argument ensues, and during the course of it both parents refocus on the issues with each other and the teen never actually receives the deserved discipline.

It's noted that in the case of separations, divorces, and blended families, it becomes much more difficult to achieve this consistency. However, it's necessary for the sake of the teen; parents in the same home must come to an agreement about discipline. Parents in separate homes should try to get as close to an agreement as possible. Contracts come in handy under these circumstances because all parents get copies of the same rules and the same consequences to enforce, leaving everyone on the same page.

2. **Among Siblings**: It's equally important to treat each child the same when it comes to the disciplinary action process. In business, companies (and managers within companies) can be sued for not treating employees the same in the disciplinary action process. This is called unfair employment practices and, if proven, carries severe penalties and potentially criminal charges for the managers involved.

The point here is for your teens to understand that your parenting rules are the same for all. No one gets favored treatment. That's why the contracts make it so much easier to enforce the rules. There are no "surprises" or "that's *so* unfair" when you take the phone away or revoke privileges.

Unfair employment practices, like having inconsistent disciplinary practices, will create a hostile work environment. It's the same when you have inconsistent disciplinary practices for your children. You must treat your "little angel" in the exact same way that you treat your "problem child" when it comes to the consequences of violating the rules at home. If you don't, you will do more harm than good. You will be alienating one of your children by treating him/her more harshly and enabling the other by not allowing him/her to experience the full consequences that should result.

Using a formalized system that spells out the rules of engagement like "The Cell Phone and Social Media Contract," the "Cell Phone Only Contract," or the "Social Networking and Internet Only Contract" that clearly states the code of conduct and the consequences for any violation is an excellent method of ensuring consistency between parents and among siblings. The warning notices (there are four stages of warning notices with different degrees of consequences) are also helpful with this important process. However, using a formalized system is not worth the paper it's written on if you aren't prepared to enforce the consequences of the contract.

Location-Based Social Networks

Foursquare is one of the first location-based social networks, a popular social network that's grown to four million users in just two years, adding 100,000 new users every week. Foursquare has spawned a plethora of other location-based applications such as Facebook Places, Gowalla, Twitter, Loopt, Fabulis, Whrrl, Mytown, and at least a dozen others.

Location-based sites like Foursquare and Facebook Places allow anyone who has an account to "check in," which tells everyone where they are on a real-time basis.

Once you download the Foursquare application onto your mobile device, or whichever social network you belong to on your mobile phone, you can add your photo and then automatically link your account to your address book, Twitter account, etc. Due to the easy accessibility of your mobile phone's built-in "GPS identifier," which allows your exact location to be determined, you are now able to use these social networks to "check in" practically anywhere in the world.

The Scary Facts About Location-Based Software

Here's the problem with location-based social networks as they relate to children. When you "check in" (check ins include your profile picture and the address of your exact location), you're instantly telling those who are members of the same network *exactly* where you are. Friends, ex-friends, strangers, and bad people will know where you are right, down to how many feet you are standing away from them, if they're in your network.

The last thing you want your fourteen-year-old to do is "check in," instantly letting strangers know exactly where she is and who she's with and what she looks like (her picture will be posted next to her check in). Talk to your children about "check ins" and explain why they won't be allowed. If they have a Facebook or Twitter account, they already have the ability to check in by using the application that's already been updated on their cell phone. To block your teenager's ability to "check in" on Facebook Places, go to the Facebook chapter and look under Facebook Places to obtain the step-by-step directions.

Alarmingly, children enjoy "checking in" wherever they are; while they're at home, at school, or out having fun. By doing this, your child is letting potentially dangerous intruders into their world, essentially telling them that they're not at home, so it's OK to rob their house, or worst-case scenario, they end up being taken away from home or from the location where they've "checked in."

The news is reporting more and more serious crimes that are being committed from information gained by updates that have been posted on location-based social networking sites. The bad news is that these types of incidents are growing as the number of people using this technology increases.

Unfortunately, there is a lack of awareness about the capability of location-based technology and the risks associated with it. The dangers continue to grow as more and more people "check in" without thinking about the potential consequences. Online predators of all types use the information from location-based networks to take advantage of others.

It's very important for every family member to make sure their privacy settings are correctly set. I suggest you either eliminate or restrict the use of these applications for your teens. Even if your account is set to private, never announce to your network that you're leaving on vacation for the week or post similar updates that tell your "friends" that you're not at home. If you do, you're leaving yourself exposed and open to potentially dangerous situations.

Twitter

As of June 2010, Twitter had over 190 million monthly users—which is unbelievable growth since it launched the company in 2006. It's gained substantial popularity around the world, especially among users that are over eighteen years old.

Twitter is a social networking and micro-blogging site all rolled up into one news and information network that asks users: "What's happening?" The site allows users to post their updates, as long as they stay with the 140 characters allowed for each post—also known as a tweet. Twitter also allows you the ability to "check in," so have the discussion with your child that "checking in" is against your rules.

Like most social networking sites, people find ways to use technology as a vehicle to destroy, threaten, or bully others. Because Twitter users primarily operate within the public domain, and all posts and updates are searchable by Google, the most important thing for teenagers who use Twitter to know is to make sure their site is private, which protects their tweets. You can click the box "protect your tweets" in the settings tab at the bottom of the page. But know this: even if their posts are protected, their friends' messages to them and about them are still public and available for everyone to see.

Parent's Guide Tip: Tweets are publicly visible by default. Advise your children to never reveal their location or provide details about their plans on Twitter.

Facebook vs. Twitter

Facebook is considered to be more of a *social networking* site and Twitter is considered to be more of a news and information networking site. Facebook is a closed network and Twitter isn't. Users get to decide who can see their Facebook page, and with Twitter, anyone and everyone can view your pages. Facebook gives you the ability to limit who sees your updates, photos, videos, or links that get posted to your profile.

Twitter has two privacy options; to protect or not to protect. If you "Protect Your Tweets" the people you approve to follow you will be able to access your posts. Otherwise, whatever you post is fair game and can be seen by anyone online. Since so many people are on Twitter to spread a message, very few people protect their tweets.

Facebook has more privacy options than Twitter does, which makes it easier to keep private things private on Facebook.

Twitter can be used to stream video, attach private information, and update your location all with just one-click. Instantly, your update is available for the entire world to see unless tweets are protected.

Take a look at the difference in age of the users between the ages of thirteen and seventeen for both Facebook and Twitter—Facebook is favored by more teenagers than Twitter!

Facebook		Twitter	
Ages	Users in Millions	Ages	Users in Millions
55+	35	55+	9.54
45–54	60	45–54	18
35–44	130.5	35–44	28.6
26–34	115	26–34	31.8
18–25	145	18–25	13.7
13–17	55.5	13–17	4.2

Facebook has a substantially larger percentage of underage users within their total number of active users, which is why we don't hear about teens abusing Twitter's technology as often as we hear about Facebook abuse.

Broadcast Yourself on YouTube

YouTube has made it possible for anyone with an Internet connection to post a video that a worldwide audience can watch within a few minutes. The wide range of topics covered by YouTube has turned video sharing into one of the most important parts of our Internet culture.

YouTube (owned by Google) is a video sharing and hosting website where users can upload, share, and view videos. Created in 2005, YouTube has become the dominant provider of online video in the United States, with a market share of around 43 percent and more than fourteen billion videos viewed on a monthly basis. According to the Alexa rankings in 2010, YouTube was ranked as the third most visited website on the Internet, behind Google and Facebook.

Most of the content on YouTube has been uploaded by individuals, although media corporations have also posted their content on the site. What's YouTube's slogan? "Broadcast Yourself."

You don't have to be a registered user to watch videos, but you must register before you are permitted to upload videos on YouTube's site. Videos that are considered to contain potentially adult by nature or offensive content are only available to registered users eighteen years old and up. Children know this, so when they register for an account, they state their age is eighteen years or older.

YouTube has faced a lot of criticism over the offensive content in some of its videos. The uploading of videos containing defamation, pornography, and material encouraging criminal conduct is prohibited by YouTube's rules. Unfortunately, that doesn't stop people from posting things that are against the rules. Just a few examples of controversial areas for videos include conspiracy theories, religion, Holocaust denial, and the Hillsborough Disaster, in which ninety-six football fans from Liverpool were crushed to death in 1989.

One of the problems with abuse on YouTube is that the company relies only on its users to flag content of videos if they are deemed inappropriate. A YouTube employee will view a flagged video to determine whether it violates the site's terms of service. Many are not happy with YouTube's system for policing its videos and have argued that proactive review of content should be standard practice for sites hosting user-generated content.

YouTube defends their lack of front-end screening by stating, "We have strict rules on what's allowed and a system that enables anyone who sees inappropriate content to report it to our 24/7 review team and have it dealt with promptly." Because YouTube only reviews content that's been reported, it could take time to get to an inappropriate video of your teenager deleted. This is the main reason why you need to proactively moni-tor all video recording devices (including webcams built into computers) that your teen has access to. If your teen posts inappropriate content on YouTube, have them im-mediately remove it.

Skype

Skype is an inexpensive (mostly free) technology that lets you keep in touch around the world. Skype is a software application that allows users to make voice calls over the Internet. If users on both ends of a call have webcams, you are able to see the person you are speaking to. Calls to other users within the Skype service are free, while calls to landline or cell phones are not. Make sure your child never answers a call from a Skype stranger. This happens often with Skype, so make sure they are very careful.

There are some very important things you need to know about Skype:

➢ Your Skype profile can be seen by everyone else on Skype, so don't share private information.

➢ Don't add pictures to your profile, especially your child's.

➢ Do not put details in your profile that you do not want to be publically available.

➢ You don't have to fill in your profile if you do not want to.

➢ You can change your profile at any time.

If your teen sets up a Skype account, they need to be careful with the information they include in their profile. Predators can target any Skype user over the Internet by calling their profile and hoping the other user will answer.

When I first signed up for my Skype account, I was constantly being contacted by strange and unknown screen names (mostly sexual by nature) who were using Skype to call me through our mutual public Skype accounts.

Password Protection

Make sure your teens keep their passwords private and store them where they can't be located by their friends. Teach your children never to give their passwords to anyone and to use different passwords for each of the sites they belong to. Kids don't think that their "best friend forever" today may turn out to be their worst enemy tomorrow, so you've got to be persistent.

> **Parent's Guide Tip:** Many teenagers DON'T have all of their privacy settings on "private."

The Great Digital Divide

The biggest reason that parents have difficulty managing, monitoring, and controlling their child's online activities can be summed up in four words: The Great Digital Divide.

Most parents think that their children waste their time spending so many of their free hours online. Parents also think that every minute they spend social networking or playing online games is causing their brain cells to "melt."

When children are confronted by their parent's concerns about spending too much time on the Internet, they immediately feel they're completely misunderstood— "you just don't get it, Mom"—and feel alienated by your reaction. This lack of ability to understand each other usually results in a breakdown of communication, power struggles, and a lack of understanding on both sides.

If only it was as simple as just taking away their cell phones, computers, Internet, and whatever else they use to gain access to our digital world, things would be much simpler . . . but that's not the reality we live in today.

• •

The use of technology will not be the same for all children. Your child's choice will tend to reflect his or her personality. Social butterflies tend to be heavy texters and Facebook users. Children who are less social tend to gravitate toward online games and videos. With the powerful new cell phones that are available and the interactive experience that technology delivers, they can be constantly connected everywhere they go. While our children are at school, they are gathering in clusters, often half-engaged in conversations while texting someone across the way, watching a video, listening to music, or updating Facebook. When it comes to social media and our children, one thing's for sure. Monitoring the use of social media is difficult, but the unchecked use of their powerful technology can create a culture in which children are addicted to, at risk, and lost in a digital world.

Resources and Support

Support is available online and in your community. If your child needs someone to talk to or if you want to get involved, here are some organizations that are doing great work:

Don't Believe the Type is an Internet prevention website for teens on identifying sexual exploitation online.
Visit: tcs.CyberTipLine.com/KnowTheDangers.html

FCC (Federal Communications Commision) lists prohibited text messaging websites
Visit: www.fcc.gov/cgb/policy/DomainName Download.html

Federal Bureau of Investigation—Cyber Tip Line is the site for reporting unusual e-mail or Internet communication.
Visit: www.CyberTipLine.com

GetNetWise is a public service developed by a wide range of Internet industry corporations and public interest organizations.

Visit: www.GetNetWise.org

i-SAFE—Internet Safety Education is a non-profit foundation for internet safety education.

Visit: www.iSafe.org

The Megan Meier Foundation raises awareness, educates, and promotes positive change to children, parents, and educators in response to the ongoing bullying and cyberbullying in our children's environment.

Visit: www.MeganMeierFoundation.com

The National Cyber Security Alliance provides tools and resources to empower home users, small businesses, and schools, colleges, and universities to stay safe online.

Visit: www.StaySafeOnline.org

NCSL (National Conference of State Legislatures) lists state laws regulating online behavior or use of electronic devices.

For state laws regarding electronic communication devices on school property:

Visit: www.ncsl.org/default.aspx?tabid=17853

For state laws regarding computer harassment or cyberstalking laws:

Visit: www.ncsl.org/IssuesResearch/
TelecommunicationsInformationTechnology/
CyberstalkingLaws/tabid/13495/Default.aspx

Netsmartz is committed to keeping kids and teens safer on the Internet.

Visit: www.NetSmartz.org/Teens

Visit The Kids Site (also a good example of using games for learning).

Visit: www.NetsmartzKids.org/indexFL.htm

Wired Safety provides help, information, and education to Internet and mobile device users of all ages, handling cases of cyber abuse ranging from identity and credential theft, to online fraud and cyber stalking, to hacking and malicious code attacks. It is a cyber-neighborhood watch and operates worldwide in cyberspace through more than 9,000 volunteers worldwide.

Visit: www.WiredSafety.org

4

. . . .

Teens on Facebook

For the most part, Facebook provides a fun and safe way for users thirteen years old and up to socialize online with their friends. Teens are often lacking in social maturity, so they're the ones most at risk of falling victim to online dangers when using Facebook.

With defensive parenting and constant communication, you can teach your children about the potential dangers of social networking. You can help empower them to protect themselves from online predators, guard their personal information, safeguard their username and password, preserve their online image, and learn how to determine friends from frenemies.

If you're not exactly sure what Facebook is, what it does, or why it was developed, you're not alone. Facebook (originally named Facemash) is a social networking Internet website that was launched in 2004 by four Harvard students who roomed together in college. The site was initially launched for the use of its members who attended Harvard. Members would post photos and then asked students to choose the "hotter" person.

According to Facebook's Ads system, by mid-2010, Facebook had over five hundred million users worldwide, with over fifty million of them between the ages of thirteen and seventeen. Facebook provides a place to create your personal online community; it's interactive and as close to real-time on the Internet as it gets, which is what teenagers love about Facebook.

A Facebook favorite is the Wall, a place on your site where your friends can post messages for you and for the rest of your friends to see. Think of the Wall as a constantly changing billboard displayed in your front yard that's visible for all of your neighbors to read and comment on.

What makes Facebook so attractive? The site is very interactive, creating a real-time social experience. Teens (and adults) can become totally engaged with this incredible social network.

Parent's Guide Tip: Facebook requires users to be at least thirteen years old in order to set up an account on their network.

The World's Most Popular Social Network

Millions are joining social media sites around the world, and Facebook is the number-one preferred site to join. Now five hundred million users strong and growing,

Facebook is the largest social network site in existence, with "friends" exchanging personal information without realizing the potential consequences.

People you think are your friends today could become your worst enemies tomorrow. The inherent dangers that come with a social circle that large goes without saying, so proceed with caution.

According to a study conducted by Nielson Media in January 2010, the amount of time the average person spent on Facebook jumped to more than seven hours a month. Each American Internet user spent an average of:

➢ Facebook—7:01 a month

➢ Google—1:23 a month

➢ Yahoo—2:09 a month

➢ YouTube—1:02 a month

➢ Microsoft/Bing—1:35 a month

➢ Wikipedia—0:15 a month

➢ Amazon—0:22 a month

Even if you lump together all of the time spent on all other social networking sites, it doesn't begin to come close to the amount of time people spent on Facebook.

Depending on which survey you pay attention to, the average teen spends two to four hours a day networking online. If you consider the time spent in school, the time allocated to homework, and the time spent for sports or after school activities, you begin to realize how much time the hours spent online directly relates to your child's daily life.

Teenagers *Love* Facebook

Facebook has become *the* "must-have" social networking hotspot that most pre-teens yearn for, teenagers live by, and many adults love. Take a look at how much time teens spend on Facebook:

➢ 91 percent of teenagers have profiles on Facebook that contain all of their personal information.

➢ 54 percent of thirteen- to fourteen-year-olds have a Facebook page.

➢ Fifteen- to seventeen-year-olds spend 19.9 hours a week online.

So when you hear, "Mom, can I have a Facebook account?" you shouldn't be shocked. Some parents struggle with the answer, especially when it comes to their eleven- or twelve-year-old child who can't wait to set up their profile, "friend" their friends, post their favorite pictures, and update their status.

*A **Parent's Guide** Story Submission: "I had no idea my nine-year-old son signed up for a Facebook account. He had put all of his personal information online and hadn't set his account to 'Private.' I immediately logged in and deleted his account."*

Parent's Guide Tip: Consider setting up your own Facebook account to set a good example for your teen. Show your child you will sign and follow the "Rules of Engagement."

Only a parent knows if their child is mature enough to handle the responsibility that goes along with having a Facebook account. Remember, with just one-click, Facebook is a powerful mode of communication that has the capability to reach around the world. If you decide to say "yes," here are the ten Facebook rules you should follow:

1. Obey Facebook's age limitation of being thirteen years old to create an account.

2. Execute the "Rules of Engagement" with your children. These are also known as "The Rules of Online Safety" or the "Cell Phone and Social Media Contract."

3. Require that they give you their passwords (Facebook and cell phone) so you can monitor what's going on inside their online world on a regular basis and teach them to safeguard their password. Explain how important it is *never* to tell anyone their password, not even their best friend.

4. Teach your children how to use the "Block" and "Report" features to stop abusive behavior.

5. Frequently monitor their Facebook pages. Watch for photos, posts, bullies, and anything that doesn't seem right. Watch for "tagging" and photos that have been posted to their profile.

6. Make sure their account settings are always set on "Private" and teach your child to avoid posting private information, especially information that could lead to a physical attack. For example, addresses, phone numbers, vacation information, locations, etc. should not be posted.

7. Watch out for inappropriate photo and video posts—teach your children to think twice before posting content and require your teen to immediately delete any inappropriate content that's been posted.

8. Require that your child only accept "friend" requests from people they know, and frequently review their friends list, paying close attention to people you don't know.

9. Communicate and educate your teens about Internet safety and how to watch out for online predators that set up false profiles to attract young teens. Teach them to trust their instincts: don't carry on conversations with creepy people and delete them immediately when they come across one.

10. Discuss how "checking in" or updating using Facebook Places is dangerous and is completely off-limits.

Whatever you do, don't forget to execute the "Rules of Engagement" contract at the back of this book, or use the downloadable version available inside the One-Click Safety Kit at www.oneclicksafetykit.com. The contract covers all of the types of social media hazards for teens that you need to know to keep your teens safe and secure online.

Keep in mind that when the Facebook settings are all set to "private," only confirmed friends can post to your teen's Wall or contact your teen via Facebook's Chat. If you're worried that someone will make inappropriate posts or send offensive messages, you can advise your teen to ignore that person's friend request, "block" fren-

emies they may have confirmed in the past, and ignore
all strangers online.

Parent's Guide Tip: **What's posted on Facebook
stays on Facebook.** With over five hundred million
users and growing by the minute, it's time for you to
learn how to protect yourself and your family from
participating in detrimental online activities that
could change someone's life forever.

Parenting In a Digital World

Your next steps will be to monitor your teen's Facebook
account (and all other social media sites they join),
set boundaries on the amount of usage, and most importantly, to enforce the rules to which you both have
agreed. One way to monitor your child's account is to
set up your own Facebook account, learn all the ins and
outs of how Facebook works, then "friend" them, and
require they friend you back. The benefits to friending
your teen are:

> ➢ They will think twice before they post, because
> they know you're watching.

> ➢ If you're logged into Facebook, you will be able
> to see what's happening on their profile when
> something is posted—as opposed to logging in
> under their username at a later time.

> ➢ You could be invited to become friends with their
> friends that know you.

No, you don't want to spy or invade their online world, but you do need to understand what's going on in their social networking environment.

Warning: If you want to totally and completely humiliate your child, comment on their BFF's recently posted update, exchange messages with their friends, or write something embarrassing on their wall. Remember, you were once a child too, and these types of exchanges will break down trust between the two of you—not to mention embarrass them in front of their 578 Facebook friends. The drawbacks of "friending" your children are:

➢ It's embarrassing and "not cool" for your teen to have Mom or Dad as a "friend."

➢ You won't necessarily be able to see everything that is posted or said, because they have the ability to limit what you see.

It's important that you know how much time your teen is spending online. Check in every once in a while and look over your teen's shoulder when he or she is on the computer. Ask if anything interesting is going on and be there to listen and discuss anything that might become an issue. Many parents of young teens don't allow social media sites to be used unless the computer is in a family room or main area of their home, making monitoring easier.

For a parent, knowledge is power. If you monitor your child's social networking site(s) on a daily basis, you'll get to know who all of their online friends are, who's saying what about whom, and which friends they should avoid. You'll want to make sure you periodically review their "friends" list to make sure a stranger hasn't made their way onto your child's profile.

Parent's Guide Tip: 54 percent of teens surveyed said they don't know all of their online friends.

Finding strangers that appear to be "friends" is difficult to do because teenagers have been known to lie to their parents about who their friends really are, and sexual predators typically use a fake picture as their profile photograph. A predator may look like they are a friendly seventeen-year-old teen, but in reality they may be a forty-three-year-old sexual predator who has posted a completely bogus profile in an attempt to lure children to their site.

Parent's Guide Tip: Friends = 1032: If you see that your child has an unrealistic amount of virtual "friends" that are not friends in real life, you have good reason to be suspicious.

You'll also want to review posted photos often to make sure an inappropriate picture hasn't been posted by them or someone else. If you see something inappropriate, require them to remove it right away. The longer inappropriate content stays online, the greater chance you'll have of that content finding its way to other profiles that are connected to your teen's. If that happens, it's almost impossible to get it removed.

Privacy Settings

Restrict the information that potential bullies, stalkers, strangers, or predators can get access to by helping your child set all of their privacy settings to "Private." By doing so, "non-friends" can't access information like their Wall, photos, or profile. Privacy on Facebook is controlled primarily from the "Privacy Settings" page, and it's also important to know that minors don't have public search listings created for them, so they don't appear in outside search engines like Google until they have turned eighteen years old.

Friending Your Teen Isn't Perfect

Even if you are "friends" with your child on Facebook and check their profile often, you may not be seeing everything. Why is that? Your tech-savvy teens can limit certain people (a.k.a. parents) from seeing their status updates, photos, or friends list. You'll also be excluded from Facebook Chat.

Because children typically have more social networking experience than we do, they know how to use these tools, and many of them use them to "Block" their parents from seeing what's really happening on Facebook. According to a 2010 online safety survey conducted by Nielsen:

➢ 43 percent of children say their Facebook profile picture is equally important to what they wear on the first day of school.

➢ 41 percent of parents have a rule that children have to be Facebook "friends" with their parents.

➢ 72 percent of parents say they can see their child's full profile.

➢ 67 percent of children say their parents can see everything.

➢ 30 percent said if they had the choice, they would unfriend their parents.

➢ 60 percent said they would unfriend Mom if they could.

Why pick on Mom? Moms tend to embarrass their teens by over-commenting. Bottom line, a lot of teens don't want their parents knowing too much about what's going on within their social network. They know there are always inappropriate comments or photos being posted that they can't control beyond deleting them, and they don't want you to see them.

Most teenagers have yet to realize the importance of protecting their image, which is why they would rather "die" than ask their friends to delete their inappropriate posts, pictures, or videos from their Facebook account.

> Parent's Guide Tip: 41 percent of parents say they know half or less than half of their children's online friends.

Posting Private Information

If your teen isn't careful when using Facebook, he or she might risk identity theft or even physical assault if private information is shared with a bad person that they think is a "friend." Teenagers (or adults) should never post their full name, address, social security number, phone number, current vacation or location status, or any other information that could make their profile vulnerable to sexual predators, scammers, creepers, or identity thieves.

Teach your teens that publicizing where they are going to meet friends or details about their class schedule is like openly inviting a stranger to know their daily routines. Using Facebook Places should be completely off-limits to young teenagers.

Most importantly, everything that's posted online is very public and permanent. Remind your teens that, as a rule, they should never post something online that they wouldn't want their grandmother to read. The same rule applies to photos and videos.

> Parent's Guide Tip: Vacation and location status updates should be off-limits.

Sextortion

"Sextortion" is a new term and a growing concern to watch out for.

Sextortion occurs when a person uses guilt, power, or knowledge of a certain secret to force another person into providing sexually explicit photos, having sex, or performing sexual favors.

Sextortion is one of the "crimes of choice" that Internet predators use to gain access into their target's personal life. Predators generally target teens or young adults on social networking sites like Facebook and MySpace.

Predators who practice sextortion pressure their victims to give them sexually explicit photos and/or favors in exchange for their secrecy about previously obtained private information or for a promise to hold off on future violent acts.

Take the sextortion case that happened in the Milwaukee area with Anthony Stancl, an eighteen-year-old former New Berlin High School student who is serving fifteen years in prison for sextortion. Anthony, an honor student, got more than thirty boys to send him naked photos of themselves . . . by posing as a female on Facebook. He then blackmailed several boys into performing sexual acts by threatening to share those pornographic images if they said no.

Throughout 2010 there have been ongoing acts of sextortion occurring at universities across the country. A predator preys on sorority pledges by first studying their Facebook profile and then approaching them using Facebook, pretending to be a sorority sister or an alum from their college. The first communications seem harmless to an unsuspecting freshman, yet are obvious attempts to gain trust. Subsequent Facebook chats and e-mails get creepy, with requests for naked pictures, followed by threats to reveal secrets and commit violent acts. As of December 2010, the dozen or so victims to date attend southwest schools: University of Florida, Florida State University, Auburn University, University of Alabama, and Louisiana State University. So far, several college students have actually provided their assailant with naked photos.

Out of the people who report sharing nude photos of themselves, almost a third of them have shared the photos with people they only know online or with people they've never met face-to-face. What's important about sextortion is that parents teach their children not to trust anyone online that they don't know, to keep their profile private—even after they turn eighteen years old—and to make sure they report any online contact they've received from online strangers who are asking for private or creepy information.

Teens and young adults need to understand that when they take these types of photographs or if they turn on their webcam for strangers, the person on the receiving end can easily record and spread the information anywhere they choose, or demand more and make threats if they don't receive it.

Covert Language on Facebook

Teens are now using secret Facebook language to stop parents and employers from being able to monitor their social activities such as partying and drinking. Teenagers want to share their experiences they had at the Friday night party with their Facebook friends, but they don't want their parents to know the details.

Instead of writing they are drunk, teens post "getting MWI" which stands for "mad with it." Being in a relationship is known as "taken" or "Ownageeee," and "Ridneck," a corruption of "redneck," means to feel embarrassed. This new language has been created to keep teen activities secret from parents and goes far beyond the abbreviations that are commonly used in text messaging.

➢ Guide = Experienced drug dealer

➢ Bagging = Describes the action of using inhalants in order to achieve an euphoric state of being

➢ Co-Pilot = A friend who has agreed to stay sober while the other child is taking hardcore drugs like LSD or inhalants

It's clear that the creation and use of their own social language is a deliberate attempt to keep parents and adults from understanding what is written on their Facebook profiles, and to cover up the truth about drinking, sex, drugs, or other behaviors they don't want parents or adults to know about.

> Parent's Guide Tip: Children say "It's raining candy" to describe when they are taking drugs like Ecstasy.

Secret Facebook Identities

If your child has something to hide, they might make a Facebook profile behind your back, or have one account that's parent-friendly and a separate account that's only for their friends. If they use Facebook often and they show you a profile that seems skimpy on content or not up-to-date, that should be a red flag that there might be a second account set up under a different username.

Children have been known to set up fake accounts and post mean pictures and comments to harass or threaten their intended target.

In 2009, a ninth-grade high school student was arrested for creating a website that featured embarrassing photos of a classmate and posted anonymous, insulting, and very hurtful comments for everyone to see.

Facebook Places

By using GPS technology, Facebook Places provides all Facebook users with the ability to let their friends know exactly where they are, on a real-time basis.

Here's the problem: According to a survey conducted by AOL, 54 percent of teens surveyed said they don't know all of their friends that are connected to their social network.

Facebook automatically defaults the privacy settings on Places to "friends." That's where problems can arise. It means that all the friends of the friends of the direct friends that your child has added to their site get the same information. Fifty-four percent of children surveyed will likely be sharing their current location with people they don't personally know. What this means is if we don't educate our children, *half of the teens out their will likely share their location with people they don't know.*

Think about this for a second . . . just a few years ago, society would have found the idea of teenagers revealing and sharing their current location with people they don't personally know to be insanity, yet it's an accepted practice with all of the location-based social networking sites that provide the ability to "check in."

The good news? It's easy to fix—just follow the steps below. Next, tell your teenagers it's unacceptable for them to "check in" on Facebook Places, or any other "location sharing" network, and explain the dangers inherent with "checking in." The BIG problem with this technology is that most parents don't know that Facebook Places exists or what it does.

If you want to block Places, try this:

1. Click Account (top right hand side of screen) to bring up menu options, choose Privacy Settings.

2. On the settings page scroll to bottom and click Customize Settings.

3. On the "Places I Check In To" tab, it will probably be set to Friends only—click the arrow next to it and choose Customize.

4. On the Custom privacy window that pops up, next to Friends Only click the arrow and choose Only Me.

5. Scroll further down and disable the option that allows friends to check you/them in.

6. Click Save Setting. That's it. You're done; you don't need to click anything else as it's now saved.

I recommend you "check in" on Places right now. This way, you'll know exactly how it works and you'll be able to explain the downside of this technology to your children. Expect some pushback from your teens for not being able to use this feature, as most of them think it's cool to let everyone know when they're at the movies or when they're at a party.

Important Note: Never set your (or your child's) master privacy controls to "Everyone," and be sure to turn off the ability for friends to check your child in. To do this, go to the Facebook Privacy Settings in Places and turn off the setting to "Let Friends Check Me In."

If someone ends up checking your teen in somewhere, teach them how to remove any Facebook Places check in or tag—using their mobile device or by going online. This is like removing themselves from a photo tag, which I'm confident they already know how to do.

Blocking on Facebook

It's important you know how to "Block" someone on Facebook and that you teach your children how to do so as well. If they already know how to "Block," advise them to get used to using the feature more often. Your teen can use the "Block" feature to prevent all interactions with someone they no longer wish to interact with. If your teen receives inappropriate or abusive communications, they can "Block" the person who's posting this information from being able to post anything in the future.

Parent's Guide Tip: Your teen can "Block" someone on Facebook without the person they are blocking knowing that they've been blocked. Facebook does NOT notify anyone when a "Block" is requested.

Reporting Inappropriate Content

If you or your child comes across inappropriate content or offensive material on Facebook, you can report the offender. Facebook takes the safety of its users seriously and makes a significant effort to take down any objectionable material that may be posted on the site. Facebook also encourages users to report offensive profiles, messages, groups, events, shares, notes, videos, and photos. Reported items are reviewed by Facebook administrators and removed if deemed in violation of their Statement of Rights and Responsibilities policy.

It's important for you and your teens to know that all reports of abuse on Facebook are confidential. The user who is reported will not know that you have reported them. Facebook doesn't guarantee they'll remove the reported content after the investigation is complete, but they do promise that any violation of their Statement of Rights and Responsibilities policy is cause to either remove the abuse that was reported, or users who repeatedly violate their Statement of Rights and Responsibilities policy can be permanently banned from the Facebook site.

> **Parent's Guide Tip:** It's a good idea to recommend that your child block and report strangers who have landed on their profile by friending mutual "friends."

Online Branding and Image Protection

Teach your child about personal branding as soon as their first social networking account is opened. Personal online branding and image protection is not taught in our schools, nor is it mentioned in any Facebook literature; yet, it's one of the most important things our children need to know about networking online. It's up to parents to teach their children that their reputations are at stake with each keystroke they make. Our children must learn to build their reputations in a positive way—online and off.

Managing and monitoring an online profile is part of personal branding and image protection, and it's a good thing to do at any age. For children, it happens like this: "My friends tagged me in an update. I don't like it because it's rude and makes me look like a bitch, but I don't want to look bad by untagging myself." Peer pressure just went to a whole new level on Facebook.

Teach them it's not bad etiquette to un-tag themselves from notes, pictures, videos, or essentially anything that they don't agree with or that makes them look bad. Teach your child that it's OK to request anyone to remove their picture from any social network, especially if it disparages their image in any way.

Even as adults, we may feel uncomfortable doing this, so just think how much harder it is for children to make those types of requests from their online friends. Children risk looking "un-cool" with their friends and starting gossip and drama by asking a so-called "friend" to have content taken down from Facebook. More often than not, you'll find that teens end up leaving the comments or photos posted in order to avoid the risk of losing friends.

It's up to you to empower your teen to take personal responsibility and act proactively—after all, it's *their* reputation that is at risk!

Think No One's Watching?

Think again. College admission counselors, coaches, teachers, school administrators, camp counselors, and prospective employers are all looking at Facebook to check references. As an employer myself, our human resources department checks all potential employees to see what their Facebook profile looks like. It's up to you to explain to your children that their status updates are not for their friends' eyes only.

> **Parent's Guide Tip:** Convince your child that the Internet is not a personal venue like a diary is.

Children are smart; they just don't always think things through as they should. They also know perception matters. They just don't know how *much* it matters until they find out they didn't get that job they were applying for because of an inappropriate comment, photo, or Facebook post. Whatever you do, when you start making recommendations about content posts, don't let them comfort you with "It's private, Mom!"

Privacy settings on social networking sites are notorious for glitches. And, remember the "six degrees of separation"? It still applies—more so than ever with Facebook. The list of "mutual friends" who can access your child's information is thousands of people long, even if they only have 150 friends.

Tag—You're It!

Well, sort of. One of the most popular features on Facebook is tagging, which gives you the ability to identify and reference people in photos, videos, and notes. Sometimes that includes referencing friends, groups, or even events they are attending—for instance, posting "Grabbing drinks with Samantha Jones," or "I'm heading to Starbucks—anyone want a latte?"

Friends you and your teen tag within status updates will receive a notification and a Wall post linking them to your post. They will also have the option to remove tags of themselves from posts. Tagging is a difficult concept to grasp unless you have experienced it for yourself. If you have a Facebook account, have your teen tag you in one of their status updates, and you'll quickly understand the power of Facebook tag.

Parent's Guide Tip: If your child gets "tagged" in an unfavorable photo, explain how important it is for them to stay in control of their image—not someone else.

Consider This: A photo of your fifteen-year-old daughter in her bathing suit with a bunch of other bikini-wearing teenagers gets posted on a social media site by one of her friends . . . and your daughter gets tagged. It's a photo you would never want the world to see, but it's been posted for five days before it catches your attention. Having your daughter un-tag herself seems like a simple solution—but you quickly realize that since her photo has been online for days on pages you don't control, you've lost the ability to stop people from sharing and labeling her picture across the Internet.

Parent's Guide Tip: In the Facebook privacy settings, be sure to change who is permitted to view images with your child in them.

Reporting Abuse on Facebook

The best way to report abusive content on Facebook is to use the "Report" link that appears nearest to the content itself. When a report is submitted, Facebook will review your request and take any action warranted by their Statement of Rights and Responsibilities policy. Here's how you report abuse:

- ➢ **Report a Profile:** Account drop-down menu available from the top of every page.

- ➢ **Report a Photo:** Go to the specific photo and click the "Report This Photo" link that appears below the photo.

- ➢ **Report an Inbox or Email Message:** View the message and click the "Report Message" link that appears below the sender's name. Note that you can only report messages from non-friends.

➢ **Report on a Group or Event:** Go to its main page and click the "Report" link that appears below the group or event.

➢ **Report a Page:** View the Page and click the "Report Page" link that appears in the left column below the Page photo.

Whenever you or your child reports someone, Facebook also recommends that you consider "blocking" the user who you're reporting. People you block won't be able to find you in searches, view your profile, or contact you with pokes, Wall posts, or personal messages. You can block people by adding their names to your Block list at the bottom of the Privacy Settings page, or by checking "Block This Person" when you report them.

Parent's Guide Tip: Anyone your teen reports won't be notified and any existing ties they have to the person they are reporting will be removed.

Games and Apps

Most of the games and applications on Facebook are aimed and advertised directly toward teens. Most teenagers don't realize (or care) that these games and applications are not part of Facebook. Rather, they are developed by third party vendors and are *not* subject to the same privacy settings and terms of service as Facebook.

Watch out for the applications that contain external downloads, as they could contain viruses. Sunbelt Software has reported several suspicious Facebook scams, from a Texas Hold'em poker application containing adware to various phishing scams.

Make sure you have an up-to-date antivirus program and ad-blocking software (like McAfee) that can catch these types of online threats. Talk to your children about reviewing the terms of service and privacy policies for apps before they accept any downloads. Also, advise them to never open a link posted on their wall from someone they don't know, as it could point to a malicious site or phishing scam.

Stranger Danger!

In early 2010, Peter Chapman, a thirty-three-year-old registered sex offender, was sentenced to life in prison for kidnapping, raping, and murdering a seventeen-year-old girl he met through Facebook. Chapman had created a fake Facebook profile and pretended to be seventeen years old to gain his victim's trust.

Despite Facebook's efforts to rid their site of online predators, the system isn't foolproof. The company has banned convicted sex offenders from joining Facebook, and in 2008, any known sex offenders already on the site were removed. But, with the reality of Peter Chapman, it's clear that predators are still finding ways to cheat the system.

As I mentioned earlier, you can use Facebook's privacy settings so that your child is directly interacting only with people they know, and more importantly, you should hide information such as their age, photos, school, and full name from people who are not direct friends. If you're monitoring regularly, look for photos of strangers within their friends list, even if they look like they are your child's age.

> **Parent's Guide Tip:** Just because you have a son, that doesn't mean that he is immune to the dangers of online predators.

Stress to your child the importance of completely avoiding people they don't know in real life. Even if the stranger's profile says that they are the same age as your child and that they go to a nearby school, the profile might be a fake. A good way to tell if the "friend" is suspicious is if that person isn't connected to most of their other friends. Make sure your child reports any stranger who tries to contact them or engage in any inappropriate activity.

The Ten Facebook Rules to Live By

Before allowing your teen to get their Facebook account (or any other social networking site), follow these "Ten Facebook Rules to Live By":

1. Obey Facebook's age limitation of being thirteen years old to create an account.

2. Execute the "Rules of Engagement" with your children. These are also known as "The Rules of Online Safety" or the "Cell Phone and Social Media Contract."

3. Require they give you their passwords (Facebook and cell phone) so you can monitor what's going on inside their online world on a regular basis, and teach them to safeguard their password. Explain how important it is never to tell anyone their password, not even their best friend.

4. Teach your children how to use the "Block" and "Report" features to stop abusive behavior.

5. Frequently monitor their Facebook pages. Watch for photos, posts, bullies, and anything that doesn't seem right. Watch for "tagging" and photos that have been posted to their profile.

6. Make sure their account settings are always set on "Private" and teach your child to avoid posting private information, especially information that could lead to a physical attack. For example, addresses, phone numbers, vacation information, locations, etc. should not be posted.

7. Watch out for inappropriate photo and video posts— teach your children to think twice before posting content, and require your teen to immediately delete any inappropriate content that's been posted.

8. Require that your child only accept "friend" requests from people they know and frequently review their friends list, paying close attention to people you don't know.

9. Communicate and educate your teens about Internet safety and how to watch out for online predators that set up false profiles to attract young teens. Teach them to trust their instincts: don't carry on conversations with creepy people and delete them immediately when they come across one.

10. Discuss how "checking in" or updating using Facebook Places is dangerous and is completely off-limits.

The most important thing for parents to do is to be proactive, not reactive. This includes monitoring children's Facebook profile(s) regularly, and setting the ground rules. Above all—communicate, communicate, and communicate!

• •

The only real way to keep up with technologies like Facebook is to educate yourself, stay informed of any changes Facebook makes, communicate with your teens, and stay involved. Every parent needs to take the time to learn about Facebook and parent around the nuances of social networking in order to keep your teens safe and secure.

Facebook can be a great social media tool if you know how to use it and avoid its pitfalls. When it comes to granting your young teen access to their own account, it's up to you to tell them what's acceptable and what's not. If you don't, you will be sure to regret it.

Make sure you live by the ten rules and obey the age limitations that Facebook has set for its users in order to prepare your teens for the wild, wild world of Facebook.

Popular Facebook Terms

Admin—An admin is a person who is in charge of a group. When you create a group, you are automatically listed as both an admin and the group's creator. Admins can invite people to join the group, appoint other admins, and edit group information and content. They can also remove members and other admins.

Ads—An advertisement. Users can create Facebook Ads to market their products and ideas. Ads are not free. Visit the Help Center to learn more.

Application—Users can add applications to their profiles, pages, and groups. There are dozens upon dozens of applications to choose from. Some are built by Facebook. Most are built by external developers. Visit the Application Directory to learn more. See General Application Support for Q&A.

Blog/Web log—An online diary or column maintained by an individual. Blogs generally contain commentary, but may also contain graphic images, videos, or descriptions of events.

Cause—An advocacy group or online campaign for collective action. Any Facebook user can start one. A cause can be used to raise money or promote one's position on an issue.

Charity Gifts—This feature enables Facebook users to donate money to any of twenty-one select and specifically targeted charities. Donation amounts are predetermined and range in value from ten dollars for two blankets for people suffering from a disaster or emergency to two hundred dollars for a laptop computer for a child in a developing country.

Chat—A feature that lets users talk with friends who are online in Facebook. Visit the Help Center to learn more.

Check Ins—An opt-in way of letting people know where you are and what you're doing on a real-time basis using your cell phone and GPS technology.

Creator—The person who started and administers a cause.

Creeper—People who take advantage of the new Facebook layout to try and be part of other people's lives, read wall-to-walls, look at pictures, and comment on everything.

Creeping—An act in which one looks at a friend's/stranger's Facebook profile, pictures, and recent activity. Everyone denies their involvement in this act (when in reality most people do it, then in turn accuse someone else of doing it later).

Event—A calendar-based resource that users can add to their profiles, pages, and groups that lets them share news about upcoming affairs or social gatherings.

Facebook Connect—A single sign-on service that enables Facebook users to log in to affiliated sites using their Facebook account and share information from those sites with their Facebook friends.

Facebook Blog—The official Facebook blog where you will find hundreds of posts on a wide range of subjects.

Facebook Deals—Lets merchants offer specials to mobile Facebook users who've checked into their businesses.

Facebook ID—The ability to log into a mobile app using your Facebook ID.

Facebook Platform—The underlying systems software and application framework that developers use to build Facebook applications.

Fan—A person who has joined a page because they like what that page represents.

FBML—Facebook Markup Language is a variation and subset of HTML with some elements removed. It allows Facebook application developers to customize the "look and feel" of their applications. It lets developers build social applications on the Facebook platform.

Filters—Used to separate friends into different categories. Create your own filters using Friend Lists. You can also filter by applications, like Photos. Tour the new Facebook homepage to see where Filters are used on the profile.

Friend—A person who has joined a profile, usually by invitation.

Friend Finder—A Facebook utility that helps users find present and former friends, family, coworkers, schoolmates, and other acquaintances.

Gifts—Virtual tokens of appreciation one member gives to another.

Group—A group is not a page or profile. It is a Facebook site created by bands, companies, and other organizations to promote their activities.

Highlights—Featured photos, events, notes, and more that you don't want to miss. Stories are chosen based on those in which your friends have interacted.

Inbox—The Facebook mail application.

Insights—Facebook's answer to web page analysis. For each Facebook page, Insights tracks the number of page views, unique views, total interactions, wall posts, discussion topics, fans, new fans, removed fans, reviews, photo views, audio plays, and video plays.

Koobface Worm—A rogue application that is plaguing Facebook and other social network sites. It is spread by a link that looks like a video.

Lexicon—A Facebook tool to follow language trends across Facebook. Specifically, Lexicon looks at the usage of words and phrases on profile, group, and event Walls.

Like—A feature that appears as a link next to something you see on Facebook that allows users to let others know they appreciate that something, be it a video, a comment, or something else.

Limited Profile—A profile that allows only restricted access.

Marketplace—Facebook Marketplace is a feature developed by Facebook that allows users to post free classified ads within the following categories: For Sale, Housing, Jobs, and Other. Ads can be posted as either available and offered, or wanted.

Member—A person who has joined and participates with a group.

Mini Feed—Similar to a news feed, a Mini Feed centers around one person. Each person's Mini Feed shows what has changed recently in their profile and what content (notes, photos, etc.) they've added. Mini Feeds are sent automatically and posted to friends' profiles for all to see.

Mobile—Facebook Mobile offers multiple Facebook features for your phone, such as Facebook Mobile Texts and Facebook Mobile Uploads.

Network—A circle of friends and acquaintances that centers on a city, school, company, or military organization.

News Feed—News Feeds highlight what's happening in your social circles on Facebook. News Feeds are posted to profiles for all to see.

Notes—Notes are like mini-blogs for your profile.

Notifications—Like Mini Feeds, notifications are news feeds from friends, sent automatically as they engage in activity on their profile.

Officer—Honorary appointment. Group admins can add officers to a group. Other than holding a title, officers have no additional privileges beyond regular members. They do not have admin authority.

Pages—A page is not a profile. It may look like one, but it's not. The features and capabilities are different. It is a Facebook site intended for and created by artists, musical groups, celebrities, businesses, brands, and similar entities (not individuals). You can add pages to your profile to show your friends what you care about. Only the official representative of an artist or business can create and make changes to a page.

Photos—A Facebook application that lets users upload albums of photos, tag friends, and comment on photos.

Places—Facebook's location API allows users to publish check ins from their mobile Facebook apps. Anyone checking where their friends are on Facebook will see the latest check ins from their Facebook friends. Not recommended for usage by children.

Poke—A poke is a way to interact with your friends on Facebook. It allows one user to virtually poke another. Some consider it flirting.

Profile—A profile is not a page. It may look like one, but it's not. The features and capabilities are different. It is a Facebook site intended for and created by people who want to share information about themselves and socialize with others. A profile displays a user's personal information and their interactions with friends. Each registered user may have only one profile.

Publisher—Use publisher to publish your status, photos, notes, and more into the stream. Posts show up both in your profile and on your friends' home pages.

Reporting—Involves reporting someone to Facebook for inappropriate or bad behavior(s).

RSS—Really Simple Syndication—Wikipedia defines it as a family of web feed formats used to publish frequently updated works—such as blog entries, news headlines, audio, and video—in a standardized format.

Stalker—Someone who is obsessed with someone else and stalks them on Facebook. Not always traceable or noticeable, but clues are: wall posts replying to every status update, viewing every posted picture of the person being stalked, etc.

Static FBML—A Facebook application that lets users customize their pages using Facebook Markup Language (FBML). See the Static FBML page for more information.

Status—A micro-blogging feature that allows users to inform their friends of their current whereabouts, actions, or thoughts.

Stream—The stream shows you posts from your friends in real-time. This keeps you up to date on everything that's happening. You can control who appears here.

Super Log-Off—Involves deactivating your Facebook every time you log on or off. This doesn't delete the account—that's the point. When you log back in, you'll be able to reactivate the account and have all of your friend connections back. But when you are not logged in, no one can post messages on your wall or send private messages or browse your content.

Tabs—Tabs mark the different sections of a profile. The Info tab displays basic information like birthday and hometown, as well as interests and activities. The Info tab also lists all groups to which the user is a member and all the pages to which the user is a fan. The wall tab displays the user's interactions with friends (comments and messages) as well as status messages. The photos tab displays profile photos and albums. The boxes tab displays all of the applications and features not showcased elsewhere on the profile. Other tabs: Users can feature their applications by creating a tab unique to that application.

Tag—Marking a photo or video with text that identifies the image or the person in the image.

Translations—A Facebook application that allows translators from around world to translate Facebook into different languages.

Updates—News feeds sent to you from pages that you have joined.

Video—A Facebook application that lets users share videos on Facebook. Users can add their videos with the service by uploading video, adding video through Facebook Mobile, and using a webcam recording feature. Additionally, users can "tag" their friends in videos they add, much the same way users tag their friends in photos.

Wall—A featured section inside a Facebook profile. It's a space on every user's profile page that allows friends and users themselves to post messages for all to see.

Warnings—Notices from Facebook that you have engaged in a prohibited activity or that you have reached a limit that suggests you were using a feature at a rate that is likely to be abusive.

Whitewalling—Involves deleting everything as it comes into your profile.

5

· ·

The Truth about Cyberbullying

Were you ever picked on or bullied when you were a child?

When I ask this question during my radio interviews and speeches, the answer is almost always "Yes!" Most of us would agree that being bullied is not only unpleasant, it leaves a permanent scar that is ingrained into our memories.

Today, bullies take advantage of technology to target their victims. They now have the ability to leverage the Internet and mobile devices to intensify their intent to threaten and harass to a degree that is far beyond anything we could have imagined when we were children.

In the event you are unsure what cyberbullying is, the long definition is "any cyber-communication or publication posted or sent by a minor online, by instant message, e-mail, website, diary site, online profile, interactive game, handheld device, cell phone, game device, digital camera or video, webcam, or use of any interactive device that is intentional and intended to frighten, embarrass, harass, hurt, set up, cause harm to, extort, or otherwise target another minor."

> **Parent's Guide Tip:** "Cyberbullying" is when a minor uses technology as a weapon to intentionally threaten or hurt another minor.

The act of cyberbullying requires that the Cyberbully intends to do harm to or torment their target. The exception is when a minor is careless and hurts another minor's feelings, which is called "inadvertent cyberbullying." In this case, the target feels victimized, even if it is not the other child's intention.

Cyberbullying is only between minors. If there are not minors on both sides of the communication, it is considered "cyber harassment," not cyberbullying. For example, when a minor harasses an adult, it falls under cyber harassment.

With 42 percent of teens admitting to cyberbullying and 39 percent using social networking sites to bully online, it's critical that parents realize that cyberbullying is a reality in today's society, and that it's time to take action to help facilitate change. The use and abuse of technology by those who prey on others is increasing at an alarming rate, and unsuspecting or unprepared children are easy targets for online bullies to attempt to destroy their sense of self.

Parent's Guide Tip: When it comes to children harassing other children online, you'll find the bullies' weapons of choice are cell phones, Facebook, and posting videos on YouTube.

Cyberbullying takes many forms, like physical threats, harassment, and name calling, and through more indirect acts, such as gossiping or excluding an individual. No matter what form online bullying takes, your child is likely to feel depressed, hurt, alone, and in need of your support.

Parent's Guide Tip: Keep your kids safe by understanding the dangers of social media, and help them follow some simple rules that will keep them out of online trouble.

Cyberbullying is especially damaging because of the frequency and severity with which it occurs. That's why it's critical that you try to quickly catch any type of harassment or threatening online comments that are directed toward your child. It's important for all parents to understand that the act of cyberbullying is becoming more common every day, and that no child is immune to the sting of a cyberbully.

How Does Cyberbullying Work?

Cyberbullying falls into one of three categories.

1. Cyberbullying involving direct attacks

2. Cyberbullying-by-proxy attacks

3. Public posts, updates, and broadcasting of humiliating content or images

Direct Attacks

Direct attacks are when messages are sent by instant messages, direct messages, online posts and comments, electronic mail, or harassment by text message. Examples of direct attacks by cyberbullies:

➢ When children send hateful or threatening messages to other children without realizing that, even if not said face-to-face, unkind or threatening messages are hurtful, harmful, and very serious.

➢ When children gang up on their target by sending thousands of text messages to their victim's mobile device, resulting in what's referred to as a "text attack."

➢ When a child uses the "Report Abuse" tool that is available on most social networking sites to report the victim for doing something they never did, leading to the victim's termination from the site.

➢ When a child creates a screen name that is very similar to the victim's name and then posts inappropriate things to other users that the victim never said, attracting drama and trouble.

➢ When children send death threats.

Stealing Passwords

This occurs when a child steals another child's password and converses with other people, pretending to be the other child whose password was stolen. Mean things that offend and anger this person's friends are then posted, causing online turmoil. Examples of stealing passwords by cyberbullies:

➢ When a child steals the password of another child and then locks the victim out of his or her own account so they can't get in.

➢ When a child uses another child's password to change his or her profile to include sexual, racist, and inappropriate comments or status, which attracts unwanted attention or offends others to start an intentional online war.

➢ A stolen password can result in false or fraudulent purchases, lost credits, points, or "loot" within online games.

Spreading Photographs and Videos

This occurs when children send text messages or e-mails to other people that include a sexually explicit or degrading photo or video of other children. Once an e-mail like this is sent, it is then forwarded around to hundreds of other people. This content is then uploaded to a social media site like Facebook or YouTube. Examples of spreading photos and videos by cyberbullies:

➢ When children receive sexually explicit or degrading pictures or videos directly on their cell phones and they forward them to anyone or everyone in their address book.

➤ When children take pictures or videos of someone changing in a locker room, or using the bathroom or dressing room, and then post the photo or video online for everyone to see.

Internet Polling

Who's hot? Who's not? Who is the biggest slut in the eighth grade? These are the types of questions that are being asked by cyberbullies who are using Internet polls to attack their victims. Most of the time, offensive questions are asked about victims in an attempt to destroy their reputation or make fun of them.

Online Gaming

Many children are playing interactive games on gaming devices such as Xbox 360, Sony PlayStation 3, Nintendo DS, and Sony PSP. Games that allow for play online often allow children to communicate with anyone they find themselves matched up with while playing the game. Bullies verbally abuse other teens who are also gaming online with them.

Sending Porn and Spam

This occurs when cyberbullies sign up their victims for spam on purpose, typically using pornographic websites as their weapon of choice. The bully signs up their victim as an interested party on a multitude of adult websites, which will then invite spam and thousands of e-mails from pornographic sites directly toward their intended victim.

Impersonation/Posing

A cyberbully can do considerable damage by posing as a victim and using the victim's name. For instance, they may post provocative messages in a hate group's chat room or on their social media site, inviting an attack against the victim, often giving the name, address, and telephone number of the victim to make the hate group's job easier. A bully will impersonate a target and then send messages to others saying hateful, cruel, or threatening comments while pretending to be the victim.

Social Networking Attacks

Many bullies are using social networks such as MySpace, Facebook, and YouTube. They build a profile and share whatever they want to share with their friends. They post pictures and videos, gossip, spread rumors, exclude those they want to target, create quizzes and polls, and use anonymous networks (such as Formspring) to attack their victims. In some cases, they impersonate their victims and take over their accounts, using them to post horrific information. Then they will report them to their school, parents, or to the police for being a cyberbully.

Cyberbullying by a Third Party

Often, bullies who misuse the Internet to target others achieve their goal by using accomplices. When trouble hits, their accomplices are responsible for their acts of bullying, not the third party who instigated the situation. The third party gets away without getting caught or suffering any consequences.

The Ten Signs of Cyberbullying

Special attention needs to be paid to the ten signs of cyberbullying. Parents may notice that a cyberbullied child suddenly withdraws from social activities, seeks to avoid contact with certain children, or suffers from anxiety-driven headaches or stomachaches before going to school or engaging in an activity with others.

Because cyberbullying is a silent epidemic, it's also important to pay close attention to your child's behavior, looking for things that are not consistent with how they usually behave, such as:

1. Unexpected or random bursts of anger

2. Pattern of withdrawal, shame, or fearfulness

3. Onset of depression, anxiety, or low self-esteem

4. Persistent, vague, or unexplained physical complaints

5. Diminished social contacts and withdrawal from close friends

6. Excuses to avoid school

7. Decline in grades, falling behind in schoolwork

8. Trouble sleeping or eating

9. Drug and alcohol abuse

10. Becoming evasive when asked direct questions

Research shows that your child probably won't tell you they're being harassed online or by text message. As they grow older, they're even less likely to say anything. Why is that? Nothing is more important to our children than their cell phone or computer, and parents believe that taking away their technology will solve the problem. Children also think that parents will get in the middle of the situation by reporting the bully to teachers, other parents, or the school's administration, which, in a child's opinion, makes the problem even more difficult for them.

What can we do to help our children? By educating ourselves, we can teach our children how to "Block" numbers on their cell phones and on their social networking sites. We can monitor their technology, and we can talk openly about cyberbullies.

Steps You Can Take Against Cyberbullying

Children who are bullied and cyberbullied are often easy targets because their classmates single them out as being "different." I have received numerous stories from "cyberbully survivors" who made it through some incredibly difficult times because they were eventually able to get the support they needed. How can you help your child?

➢ Listen carefully to what your child is saying to you. Be sympathetic and stay calm. Be sure you don't place blame on them, and don't look for fault. Your child needs to know that you understand what is going on and that they can count on you for support.

➤ Teach your child the defensive measures they can take to limit online attacks, like the I/B/R program.

➤ Get professional help if you think your child needs extra support or outside advice.

➤ If your child's safety is at risk, document all of the online and/or text message correspondence, and then contact the authorities. Cyberbullying is a serious offense and is taken seriously by authorities.

➤ Keep the lines of communication open with your child and spend extra time with them. Provide extra encouragement whenever possible, and be a *friend* to your child, as well as a parent.

➤ If you suspect your child is being bullied online while they are at school, contact your child's teacher or the administration of your child's school. But, you will want to try and get your child's approval first. Ask for the school's cooperation in getting the bullying at school to stop.

➤ Always stick to the facts, write them down, and keep copies of everything.

➤ Depending on your child's age and the situation, you might be able to contact the cyberbully's parents for help.

➤ Support and nurture your child's self-confidence levels.

➢ Tell your child not to feel ashamed, that they are not alone, and to reach out to people they can trust for help.

The top eight reasons children are cyberbullied are:

1. They're physically or mentally challenged.
2. They're gay.
3. They have yet to hit their growth spurt.
4. They're smarter than most of their classmates or are considered nerdy by the "in" crowd.
5. They lack self-confidence.
6. They follow the rules.
7. They look or dress "differently."
8. They don't defend or speak up for themselves when they are bullied.

Self-Confidence is Critical

As a parent, it can be difficult to watch your child go through the struggles of adolescence. While you can't always protect your teen, staying involved is important. Several of the reasons children are cyberbullied often relate to self-confidence and self-esteem. If you can help your child improve in these areas, your child will be more likely to avoid becoming a target and, proactively, they will be able to defend against an attack by a cyberbully. Keeping the following points in mind can help you and your child make it to graduation without being the target of a cyberbully.

1. Keep on top of your teen's homework and grades. Set aside a time and place for completing assignments every night. If your teen has difficulties or needs help working up to their potential, look into tutoring programs or learning centers. They may fight it, but they will eventually appreciate the success they will achieve.

2. Being involved in extracurricular activities is a surefire way to build self-confidence. While the possibilities vary from school to school, there's an option for everyone. The musically-talented will want to try out for marching band or choir, while your family's "king debater" may want to join the debate team. Clubs and teams give teens an instant peer group to belong to, give them the satisfaction of working with others toward a common goal, and often help them develop leadership skills, all of which leads to increased self-confidence.

3. If your teen isn't interested in any of the clubs or sports offered at school, look for activities in the community, or, if they are old enough, a part-time job. Weekly dance classes, riding lessons, martial arts training, church programs, or working with the public will help your teen gain confidence. Learning to have a good work ethic, having dedication to complete a commitment made, and cooperating with others are all skills that will stay with your child long after their teenage years. Whatever choice is made, the experience will add to their level of self-confidence.

4. Volunteering is another extracurricular option. Some high school clubs, such as National Honor Society, focus on community service, but it's also possible to approach an organization like the Humane Society or a senior center and ask if they need any help. Encourage your teen to find an organization or cause in which they are interested, but don't force it. Requiring that your child volunteer in something that they are not interested in isn't truly volunteering. It becomes a *chore* and many of the "feel-good" benefits can be diminished.

5. Relationships are key to self-confidence during the teen years. While we often think of romantic relationships as causing the most difficulty, relationships with friends can be just as much trouble. Make sure that your teen is developing positive friendships, and ask to meet their friends and their friends' parents. If you feel that your teen is heading in the wrong direction, steer him or her toward more positive activities and friendships. Make sure that your teen is choosing friends for the right reasons—because they enjoy each other's company or have shared interests, not because someone is "cool" or "popular."

6. Popularity is the magic word during the teen years. Not feeling *popular* may lead to self-doubt. If you feel that your teen is having trouble fitting in, have an honest talk with him or her about how they view themselves and what they want out of their friends, school, and life in general. If your child seems to be having trouble making friends, help to get them involved in a new activity that will introduce them to other young people with the same interests. It's

so important to *emphasize* all of their great qualities and let them know that they don't have to be the homecoming king or queen to be an amazing person.

As much as teens don't want to admit it, family relationships are a very important part of their lives. Strong parental relationships are key to helping teens weather the threats of cyberbullies, peer pressure, stress, and other problems of adolescence.

Teens are notorious for not wanting to tell their parents *anything*. If you ask how school was today, you'll get a shrug and a mumbled answer. It's easy to give up in the face of this reticence, but do everything you can to keep the lines of communication open. If they know they will find support at home, teens can feel confident in even the most difficult situations, like being cyberbullied.

My Child is the Bully!

What if your child is the bully? Dealing with cyberbullying is just as important—if not more so—if you suspect that your child is actually doing the bullying. A cyberbully knows that what he or she is doing is wrong and will seek to avoid detection. They may wait until late at night to access the Internet. Conversely, when groups of cyberbullies get together, they go online and then quickly shut down their devices when a parent or adult enters the room.

Other signs of cyberbullying are multiple social networking accounts, boasting that an account had been shut down but that he or she is already "back in business," and unreasonable anger and even fury when access to the Internet is taken away in response to a broken rule.

How can you tell if your child is the bully? You'll find out by watching for signs and by monitoring their online communities such as Facebook, YouTube, etc. Read the exchanges and updates that your child is posting. If you find out your child is disrespectful to anyone or has posted hurtful comments, videos, or pictures, it's critical that you have a serious conversation with them and immediately restrict their access to all technology.

The profile of a cyberbully looks much like the profile of a schoolyard bully. A cyberbully:

- ➢ Is easily angered
- ➢ Is obsessed with explosives or weapons
- ➢ Is obsessed with violent games, TV, or literature
- ➢ Has parents who *enable* behavior by either inaction or encouragement
- ➢ Has no remorse for his or her actions
- ➢ Has tendencies to "not care about schoolwork" and has grades that are lower than they should be
- ➢ Blames others
- ➢ Has deep depression with extreme mood swings
- ➢ Has high frustration levels and poor coping skills
- ➢ Is often violent, both with words and acts, and is the instigator of physical fights
- ➢ Often resorts to name-calling, makes violent threats, acts superior to others, and feels justified in his/her behavior

- ➢ Abuses drugs, alcohol, and other substances
- ➢ Has threatened to commit or has attempted suicide
- ➢ Has been suspended or expelled from school
- ➢ Participates in gang activities
- ➢ Is cruel to animals or destroys property
- ➢ Is disrespectful to others, humiliates, and sets traps to embarrass
- ➢ Glorifies violence and intimidates others
- ➢ Has little or no support at home from caring adults
- ➢ Peers are of the same tendencies or they isolate themselves
- ➢ Has been personally abused or has witnessed abuse in the home

Consequences for Cyberbullies

All children and teens need to be disciplined if they have participated in malicious or hurtful behavior. This includes cyberbullying. Here are some tips for disciplining a teen who has cyberbullied another child. Be sure to use the One-Click Safety Kit that comes with a built in step-by-step process for dealing with cell phone and Internet violations. This can be found at www.OneClickSafetyKit.com. You should also consider taking the following actions as part of the consequence process:

Step 1: Remove Internet and cell phone privileges.

Since he or she probably used the Internet and cell phone as the source for ill-intended purposes, he/she should lose access to that technology. The length of time is up to you, but it's recommended to eliminate it for a minimum of one to two months.

If he/she needs the Internet for school research, it should be used only with a parent looking over the teen's shoulder or sitting next to him/her. I know it's going to be inconvenient, but if we don't keep control, they will just be back online again. They should lose all access to Facebook, MySpace, online games, and anything else they use to network online.

If your teen already spends a lot of time texting and on the Internet, this would be a great time for him or her to get involved with a new school activity, get a part-time job, learn a new hobby, or start reading.

When online and cell phone access is regained, it should only be done after the "Rules of Engagement" are revisited, with emphasis placed on the consequences for another misstep. It's extremely important that you always have complete access to your teen's online and text message activity. Measures should be taken to prevent your teen from ever cyberbullying again—refer to what's been outlined within the One-Click Safety Kit.

Step 2: Write an essay on the dangers of cyberbullying.

In addition to losing Internet privileges, you can have him or her write a research essay on the subject. Your son or daughter should write about the consequences of cyberbullying, why it is inappropriate, and what it must feel like to be the victim of a cyberbully.

Step 3: Assign him or her to read a book about cyberbullying.

Another great education tool and consequence you could require is to have them read a book about cyberbullying. One to consider is *Bullying Beyond the Schoolyard: Preventing and Responding to Cyberbullying* by Sameer Hinduja and Justin W. Patchin. At the very minimum, have him or her read the entire chapter on cyberbullying from this book.

Step 4: Assign him or her to participate in community service.

This isn't directly related to cyberbullying, but can help in the disciplinary process. There are many social service agencies that desperately need volunteers. Check with your child's counselor for recommendations in your community.

Step 5: Apologize and take responsibility.

You will also need your child to take responsibility for their actions by:

➤ Requiring that your child apologize in person to the child he or she has bullied.

➤ Requiring that your child write an apology letter to both the child and his or her parents. Refer to the three sample apology letters in the Resource section of this book.

➤ If your child has gotten into trouble with his or her teacher or the school administration as a result of being a bully, he or she needs to apologize to them, also.

If your child is a bully, you have the personal responsibility to teach him or her that the bad behavior will not be tolerated for any reason. Children need to understand that other people are hurt by their actions, and that it is *wrong* to hurt other children's feelings in an attempt to feel better about themselves. It's important to try to figure out why your child has turned to cyberbullying. Statistically:

➤ More than 65 percent of cyberbullies also bully in person.

➤ More than half of those have bullied the same person virtually and in person.

➤ Cyberbullies are rarely the victim of being cyberbullied.

➤ Size doesn't matter—cyberbullies don't have to be "tough" or big.

➤ Most cyberbullies have little regard or respect for others.

If you have discovered that your child is a cyberbully, ask your child why and listen to their explanation. While your child is in the wrong, you are still his or her number-one supporter, and you must listen to what your child has to say in defense of his or her actions.

Top seven reasons why children cyberbully others:

➤ Peer acceptance

➤ Peer jealousy

➤ Revenge

➤ Rejection

➤ Entertainment—just for the "fun" of it

➤ Need for power and attention

➤ Because they hate the victim

Listening leads to communication and understanding, which can lead to positive change. Sometimes, a child will use cyberbullying as a defense. Your child may have felt that in order to keep from being made fun of, it was better to cyberbully someone else instead. It may be as simple as just not liking that person. Try hard to get to the bottom of your child's anger, do your research, and don't hesitate to seek professional advice.

Bottom Line: The only way to stop a child's negative behavior is for them to understand that there will be *consequences* for their actions. That's where the various contracts that I've provided for you in the One-Click Safety

Kit will be of help. The contracts are fully adaptable to your family's needs. By having your kids help you set up the penalties to be imposed for misuse, you are no longer the bad guy.

You will also need to take control and require that your child disable all of their social media sites and limit their cell phone options so all they can do is call their parents. This includes disabling texting and any access to the Internet from their phone. You'll also need to require they apologize in person and in writing, and of course, choose whatever additional consequences you feel are appropriate for your child's behavior.

Should Our Schools Intervene?

Is it the responsibility of our educators to police our children's cell phones, home computers, and social network conversations? It's not uncommon to find that parents are asking schools to step up and protect their children from the digital warfare that's going on in cyberspace because they don't know where to turn or what they can do.

More often than not, our schools' discipline procedures have yet to address specifics like social networking slander and communication originating from cell phones. Unless an act of cyberbullying is reported, witnessed, happens on school property while using the schools technology, or a student seeks help from a teacher or an administrator, it's difficult to require that our schools intervene. Because cyberbullying is "invisible," it takes proactive parenting and constant communication with our teens to uncover any turmoil that is most likely brewing online. Schools are having a difficult time coming up with a proactive program to get students engaged in stopping cyberbullying.

Here's a prime example of the difficulty schools face: Someone stumbled on a Facebook page titled the "Southport High School Burn Book" that was pitting students against each other. The site was full of rumors, threats, and insults; children were called out by name, sexual orientations were questioned, and reputations were ruined. The site appeared to encourage fights on campus that were photographed, videotaped, and then posted to YouTube and linked/posted to Facebook. Hundreds of children stood by and watched one of the altercations, and several fed the fire by using their cell phones to record videos of the attack and post the footage online.

Facebook would *not* remove the page, but both the Facebook pages and the YouTube links were eventually taken down by the anonymous creator of the site from the pressure brought by the Southport High School students.

This is just one of the thousands of examples where the combination of technology, students, and schools collide, resulting in a nightmare for everyone. According to the National Education Association:

➤ 100,000 children carried guns to school in 2009 as a result of being bullied.

➢ 43 percent of students fear harassment in the restrooms at school (Bureau of Justice).

➢ The top five states in regard to reported incidents of bullying and cyberbullying are California, Illinois, New York, Pennsylvania, and Washington.

While cyberbullying might start from home, it can quickly move to the school environment—and many of our schools have yet to amend their policies and procedures to include acts of cyberbullying.

In my opinion, it's not *just* the schools' responsibility to monitor what's being posted by our children on Facebook, MySpace, or Twitter while they are off of school grounds, using technology that doesn't belong to the school. It's the responsibility of parents who have children under the age of eighteen to monitor their social media activities. However, if a student is caught in the act of cyberbullying or reports an incident of being bullied online while at school, the school administration should report the incident to parents, take the appropriate steps necessary to protect all of the students involved while they continue to investigate the incident, and, if necessary, report the cyberbully to the police.

Cyberbullying is on legislative agendas around the country. State lawmakers are seeking to set guidelines for schools to help them address the problem so that formal policies and procedures are in place. Cyberbullying presents a challenge for schools since the boundaries for school intervention are unclear.

Defensive Steps to Take Against Cyberbullies

Empower your child to ignore anyone who bullies or threatens them online or by text message. Teach them how to "block" anyone who has sent them inappropriate messages or posts something that is offensive. Be open and promise your child that when they come to you with a problem, your first reaction won't be to take away their technology.

Instead, let them know that you'll help them defend against online bullies with the Ignore/Block/Report Program. The program can be found in the back of this book or online at www.OneClickSafetyKit.com.

> **Parent's Guide Tip:** According to a study completed in 2010 by the Department of Justice, 43 percent of teenagers reported being victims of bullying by cell phone or through the Internet.

Cyberbullying Can End in Tragedy

Over the last few years, we have seen high profile, tragic headlines involving the consequences of cyberbullying in cases that ended in the loss of life such as those of Megan Meier, Jesse Logan, Phoebe Prince, Hope Witsell, Tyler Clementi, and Asher Brown.

➤ As of the end of 2010, over thirty children had taken their own lives after being cyberbullied.

➤ According to the Cyberbullying Research Center, about half of young people have experienced some form of online harassment and 10 to 20 percent experience it regularly.

➢ According to i-SAFE, over half of adolescents and teens have been bullied online, and about the same number of teens have engaged in cyberbullying.

➢ According to i-SAFE, over 25 percent of adolescents and teens have been bullied repeatedly through their cell phones or the Internet.

➢ According to the Cyberbullying Research Center, victims of cyberbullies are 1.9 times more likely to attempt suicide.

Vehicles for cyberbullying exist everywhere. Cell phones, computers, iPads, and anything that provides an Internet connection to our digital world can be used as a relentless and nonstop weapon for online bullying. Today it's almost impossible for a child to have a problem with another child that doesn't either start online or end up online. There are now very few "he said, she said" situations that stay face-to-face.

Despite the efforts to curtail online bullying through education, discipline, and other means, many worry that it may actually be on the rise. There are social networking sites like www.littlegossip.com that encourage children and young adults to write anonymous and obscene comments about their peers, which encourages cyberbullying. Many comments on these types of social networking sites are obscene, while others are racist, homophobic, or threatening. And what's the worst part about these networking sites? It's that our children are so willing to spread hurtful rumors about one another freely, as shown by the explosion of popularity surrounding the use and abuse of sites like littlegossip.com.

Much like traditional bullying, the cyber variety is underreported because children are afraid of retribution or afraid of bringing even more attention to themselves. Unlike traditional bullying, cyberbullying is much easier to accelerate and gains a lot more attention among youth. A cyber attack becomes viral instantly and everyone witnesses the attacks just as quickly, so it's hard to take anything back or hide from these types of attacks. For most children, when it comes to being the victim of a cyberbully, words do hurt and words do sting—and for some, words can kill.

Uneven Laws

Although invasion of privacy laws exist in every state, the application of those laws varies from state to state, and unless those cases lead to wrongful death charges or civil claims, the punishment can be fairly light, especially in regard to cases in which suicides result from humiliation caused by unwanted exposure. Over the next few years, we should see action by lawmakers across the country dealing with both physical and online bullying. For up-to-date information about the different state laws, visit the resource section at: www.ShawnEdgington.com.

Coach and Monitor

On a regular basis, you'll need to coach your children and monitor their social media accounts to help your child avoid online bullies, or to be sure that your child isn't one. It's critical that you play a role in protecting their online image until they are ready to do it themselves.

Once you begin incorporating regular social network monitoring into your daily parenting responsibilities, you'll quickly understand the ins and outs of social networking and why you are monitoring. You will probably discover how cruel, rude, and thoughtless many teens become when they are posting comments and pictures online about other people.

You might also find that your teen's Facebook account is completely out of control and in need of your special attention. This situation is more common for parents who have never monitored their teen's online accounts in the past. If this happens to you, what should you do? Have your teenager make all of the deletions and "requests to remove content" as soon as possible. Your next step will be to sit down with your child to discuss image protection, who's watching, and to execute the "Rules of Engagement" contract that details your expectations regarding social media usage, as well as the consequences that will be enforced should any rules be broken.

Parent's Guide Tip: 72 percent of middle school children report having more e-mail addresses than their parents know about.

Start Talking Now

It's common for parents to speak to their children about drugs, drinking, and sex. With the changing times and the advancements of teens' total connectivity, it's critical to add social media dos and don'ts into your regular discussions.

If you find your teen is being harassed, threatened, made fun of, or bullied, offer support and comfort no matter how upset you are. Children are often reluctant to tell their parents or their friends that they are the victim of cyberbullying because they feel embarrassed it's happening to them, or they worry that their parents will further embarrass them by going to school administration, to the parents of the bully, or to the authorities.

Children are scared that if the bully finds out that they told someone about being cyber attacked, their situation will only get worse. If your child does come to you for help, be sure to thank them for having the courage to confide in you about what's happening to them.

Remind them that they aren't alone, and that you're there for support. Emphasize that it's the bully who is behaving badly—not them. Reassure them that you will work together to figure out what to do about this difficult situation, and that you won't discuss the problem with outside sources or the assailant's parents unless your child agrees.

Sometimes it's useful to approach the bully's parents through a school official, such as a counselor. If you have serious concerns about your child's safety, you will need to contact the authorities, even if your child doesn't agree with you.

As I explained in the beginning of this book—my daughter's cyberbully attack occurred two years ago when I didn't have a clue about cyberbullying. I wish I knew then what I know now. As I look back on her experience, I know the girls who harassed my daughter were not "good" girls. They had been expelled from high school, had a long history of getting into trouble, and one of the girls had a bad reputation for beating up other girls. I also knew they had uninvolved parents, and going to the school administration was out of the question, especially since they were attending a different school than my daughter.

Looking back at my personal experience, I should have taken several defensive actions on that first day she came home from school in tears:

➢ I should have developed a contract around social media and cell phone usage before she signed up for her Facebook account.

➢ Using the parental controls feature, I should have immediately blocked the girls' cell phone numbers, which would have instantly disabled their ability to send her threatening text messages.

➢ I should have been monitoring her Facebook account daily, which I never thought was necessary.

➢ I needed to explain to her what happens when you "Block" on Facebook, and then I should have had her block the girls who were posting cruel and mean comments.

Hindsight is always 20/20, but had I taken the above actions, the bullies would have been instantly stopped in their tracks. Do you know what the worst part about this was? *I wasn't in the dark*—my daughter had been telling me what was happening to her. I'm not a clueless mother, nor was I in denial. I just didn't know what to do to help her get out of her terrible three-month nightmare.

Stop Online Harassment

Being cyberbullied on a social network does not need to happen. The better informed you are and the more you engage your children with open conversation, the better protected and empowered your family will be. Be proactive and informed about social networks, parental controls, and text message capabilities that are available. Require your children to sign a social media and cell phone usage contract, and coach and monitor their moves 24/7 until you feel your child is mature enough to make the right decisions on their own.

Most of the stories that parents have sent me about their child being textually harassed or cyberbullied have been discoveries made after the fact. This means that we, the parents, have no idea about the silent epidemic of online bullying until it's either over or it's too late.

So, when you hear me say over and over again how important it is to talk to your children about their digital life, to monitor their technology, to set rules and enforce consequences if the rules are broken, and to teach your children to "Block" on their cell phone and online, it's for your child's protection.

• •

Throughout this book, it's been my goal to help you avoid a *one-click nightmare* from occurring in your home by showing you how to take proactive, preventative, and defensive measures that you need to know in order to help your child avoid cyberbullies and predators who live and rely on cyberspace to attack their victims.

It's important to know that cyberbullying is not just an adolescent problem. Adults also experience the negative effects of cyberbullying. The good news is that adults can also follow most of the steps outlined within this chapter. If you are a victim of an online bully, you must take action as soon as possible.

Whether or not you have had a personal experience with being the victim of an online bully, the pain is real and can cause emotional damage that lasts a lifetime. To help others understand the impact of cyber-bullying I'm asking that you share your personal story. I also encourage you to share any advice or strategies that you employed to help you and your family make it through this difficult time. To share your story, go to www.ShawnEdgington.com

I hope that my experiences, both personal and professional, have helped you gain an understanding about the benefits and dangers of parenting in a digital world.

Sincerely,

Shawn Edgington

Cyberbully Resource and Support Information

Support is available online and in your community. If your child needs someone to talk to or if you want to get involved, here are some organizations that are doing great work:

Angels and Doves is a nationwide anti-bullying nonprofit organization.

Visit: www.AngelsandDoves.com

Cyberbullying Research Center is dedicated to providing up-to-date information about the nature, extent, causes, and consequences of cyberbullying among adolescents.

Visit: www.Cyberbullying.us

GLSEN is also a great organization that is working to eradicate bullying and bias in schools.

Visit: www.GLSEN.org

The Megan Meier Foundation: Raises awareness, educates, and promotes positive change to children, parents, and educators in response to the ongoing bullying and cyberbullying in our children's environment.

Visit: www.MeganMeierFoundation.com

The National Center for Bullying Prevention is helping to promote awareness and teaches effective ways to respond to bullying.
Visit: www.Pacer.org/Bullying

NetSmartz is committed to keeping children and teens safer on the Internet.
Visit: www.NetSmartz.org/Teens

The One-Click Audio Set provides parents with the complete program and information to stop online and textual harassment. This seven-disc series is full of interviews, discussions, and answers you need about the dangers of social networking and how to parent in our digital world.
Visit: www.oneclicksafetykit.com

STOMP Out Bullying is focused on reducing bullying and cyberbullying.
Visit: www.StompOutBullying.org

The Trevor Project is a twenty-four-hour national help line for gay and questioning teens. The hotline is 866.4U.TREVOR.
Visit: www.TheTrevorProject.org

··

The Parent's Guide
Resources

··

The Rules of Engagement

. . . .

Cell Phone and Social
Media Contract

I promise to utilize the Ignore/Block/Report Program if I feel I'm being harassed, bullied, or threatened by text or online. I will empower my friends and family to do the same and follow these cell phone and social media rules:

➤ I will not pretend to be someone else by creating a false profile.

➤ I will not post foul or inappropriate language on any social networking site.

➤ I will not post or view inappropriate photos/videos online because I understand they will stay on the Internet forever.

➤ If my friends use inappropriate language, I'll ask them to delete their post.

➤ I will keep all of my social networking accounts on "Private."

➤ I will never "check in" or provide anyone online with my location or address.

➤ I will not bully, harass, or be mean to *anyone* online or by text message, especially about race, religion, sexual orientation, physical disabilities, or for any other reason.

➢ I won't participate in sexting, no matter what.

➢ I will never give anyone my password—even my best friend.

➢ If I get harassed or bullied online or by cell phone, I will "Block" them from my networking sites and from my cell phone so they can't call or send texts. I will not respond to their comments, and I will report them if I feel threatened, scared, or picked on.

➢ If I get harassed or bullied online or by text message, I will tell my parents and the proper authorities.

➢ I will never accept a "friend" request from someone I don't know.

➢ For my own protection, I will not use Facebook Places, Formspring.me, or Foursquare. This protects my whereabouts and my reputation.

➢ I understand my parents or guardian will be watching what is being posted on all of my social media sites and on my cell phone.

➢ I understand Skype allows complete strangers to view my personal space like my bedroom, and I will be very careful when I use it.

➢ I will not set up a face-to-face or Skype meeting with anyone I've met online.

➢ I understand my online image and reputation are important to manage at all times.

➢ If any of my friends become a victim of harassment or cyberbullying, I promise to be a true friend and report all incidents immediately.

> I will not give out any personal information about myself or anyone in my family (including names, passwords, pictures, addresses, telephone numbers, email addresses, name or location of my school) to anyone I meet online.

> I won't use my parent's credit or debit cards online or via cell phone applications without their permission.

I will follow these rules for cell phone and social media no matter where I use a computer or any mobile device. If I fail to follow the "Rules of Engagement," I will be subject to the following consequences.

The consequences for not following the "Rules of Engagement" are:

1st Offense	Warning with no loss of phone privileges *or* loss of phone for three days
2nd Offense	Loss of phone use for one week
3rd Offense	Loss of phone use for two weeks
4th Offense Final Notice	Loss of phone use for one to six months and before phone use is reinstated, rules to be reviewed

Child: _____Date:_____

Parent(s)_____Date:_____

Talking Points Defined

. . . .

Companion to the Rules
of Engagement

Checking In—When you "check in," you're instantly telling those around you who are members of the same network that you're checking into *exactly* where you are by providing the exact address of where you are located. Members will know where you are right down to how many feet you're standing away from others in your network.

Cyberbullying—Cyberbullying involves the harassment/ terrorism of an individual, including physical, emotional, verbal, sexual, and racial teasing or torment that occurs by text message or by using social media.

Facebook Places—A location-based application that allows users to publish check ins from their mobile Facebook apps. Users "check in" using text messaging or a device specific application telling everyone in their network where they are located (using GPS technology) on a real-time basis.

Formspring.me—A social networking site that allows users to ask each other questions and post comments anonymously. It's the perfect spot to harbor cyberbullies who want to hide behind technology.

Foursquare—Foursquare is a location-based social networking website, software for mobile devices, and game. Users "check in" using text messaging or a device specific application telling everyone where they are located (using GPS technology) on a real-time basis.

Password Protection—Always keep your passwords private, and store them where they can't be located. Teach your children to never give their passwords to anyone. Don't use the same password for every site. By changing it up, you'll limit your exposure to fraud.

Sexting—Sexting is the slang term for the use of a cell phone or other similar electronic device to distribute pictures or video of sexually explicit images. It can also refer to text messages of a sexually-charged nature.

Skype—Skype is a software application that allows users to make voice calls or video chats over the Internet. Calls to other users within the Skype service are free, while calls to both traditional landline telephones and mobile phones can be made for a nominal fee using a debit-based user account system. Skype profiles are public, so never put personal information inside of your profile.

Textual Harassment—The activity of sending text messages to mobile phones that are intentionally sent to threaten, harass, or bully.

Facebook Rules

. . . .

The Ten Facebook Rules to Live By

Before allowing your teen to get their Facebook account (or any other social networking site), follow these "Ten Facebook Rules to Live By":

1. Obey Facebook's age limitation of being thirteen years old to create an account.

2. Execute the "Rules of Engagement" with your children. These are also known as "The Rules of Online Safety"or the "Cell Phone and Social Media Contract."

3. Require they give you their passwords (Facebook and cell phone) so you can monitor what's going on inside their online world on a regular basis, and teach them to safeguard their password. Explain how important it is never to tell anyone their password, not even their best friend.

4. Teach your children how to use the "Block" and "Report" features to stop abusive behavior.

5. Frequently monitor their Facebook pages. Watch for photos, posts, bullies, and anything that doesn't seemright. Watch for "tagging" and photos that have been posted to their profile.

6. Make sure their account settings are always set on "Private" and teach your child to avoid posting private information, especially information that could lead to a physical attack. For example, addresses, phone numbers, vacation information, locations, etc. should not be posted.

7. Watch out for inappropriate photo and video posts— teach your children to think twice before posting content, and require your teen to immediately delete any inappropriate content that's been posted.

8. Require that your child only accept "friend" requests from people they know and frequently review their friends list, paying close attention to people you don't know.

9. Communicate and educate your teens about Internet safety and how to watch out for online predators that set up false profiles to attract young teens. Teach them to trust their instincts: don't carry on conversations with creepy people and delete them immediately when they come across one.

10. Discuss how "checking in" or updating using Facebook Places is dangerous and is completely off-limits.

IMPORTANT: Facebook requires users to be at least thirteen years old to set up an account.

Ignore/Block/Report

· ·

The I/B/R Program

The Ignore/Block/Report Program was developed as a direct result of my teenage daughter being harassed and bullied on her cell phone and on Facebook for months. The Ignore/Block/Report program helps parents and children neutralize and defend themselves against bullies who harass, threaten, or bully by text message or online.

Talk to your kids and teach them the simple three-step process:

1. IGNORE—Don't respond, and make a copy of the message if you feel it's necessary.

2. BLOCK—Call your wireless provider or go online to have the number blocked.

3. REPORT—Report the harassment to parents and the police when necessary.

Textual harassment is an unfortunate reality that has developed as a result of the growth and popularity of texting. Online harassment has grown to such a degree that special laws have been put in place to contain the problem.

As these laws will vary from state to state, you should check to see if the state where you live has such a law. In many states a single unsolicited text message that threatens physical harm or is obscene is enough to meet the definition of textual harassment.

For more information about the different state laws that govern electronic harassment, cyberstalking, and cyberbullying, visit the National Conference of State Legislatures (NCSL).

Visit: http://www.ncsl.org/default aspx?tabid=20753

Apology Letters

· ·

Sample Apology Letters for Cyberbullies

Has your teen recently participated in malicious cyberbullying behavior? Are you a parent or a school counselor helping a teen apologize for cyberbullying? If either of these is the case, it's time to apologize. An apology letter can help a victim of cyberbullying with the healing process. Though unfortunately teens can't turn back time, they can admit to their mistakes.

Sample Letter #1

Dear Marissa,

I am very sorry for my cyberbullying behavior. It was wrong and I should not have done what I did. I truly regret my actions.

I sincerely apologize. I know that no one deserves to be treated that way. I understand my behavior was very hurtful to you.

I promise never to bully you again and I will not participate in any cyberbullying in the future. I am sorry for my mistakes and poor choices.

Sincerely,

Jenna

Sample Letter #2

Dear Joey,

I am writing this to apologize for my behavior. It was wrong and I am truly sorry that I cyberbullied you. I regret my poor choices and I will not let it happen again.

I know that this behavior was very harmful. There is no excuse for what I did and I hope that my actions will not continue to cause you pain.

I know that cyberbullying is very wrong. I promise not to participate in any further cyberbullying behavior.

Please accept my apology,

Ed

Sample Letter #3

Dear Jenny,

I am truly remorseful for being a cyberbully. I am sorry and I know that it was wrong. I sincerely regret my actions and poor choices.

I know that I cannot undo the harm I have caused you. I wish I had never done it. There is no excuse for my behavior. I can assure you that I will never cyberbully you again and will never participate in any future cyberbullying.

I'm sorry,

Michael

Please note that it is not necessary for the cyberbully to recount actions in the letter. In fact, it's best to avoid doing so, as that can cause more pain. The letter should simply apologize for the behavior and respectfully convey that it was wrong. These sample apology letters are not meant to be copied word-for-word but to help in writing a letter. An apology letter should be handwritten and it can be snail-mailed or given in person.

Resources and Support

Links and Websites

Support is available online and in your community. If your child needs someone to talk to or if you want to get involved, here are some organizations and resources that provide good information:

Angels and Doves is a nationwide anti-bullying nonprofit organization.
Visit: www.AngelsandDoves.com

ComputerCOP is a quick way for parents to monitor what their children are doing online.
Visit: www.ComputerCop.com

The Cyberbullying Research Center is dedicated to providing up-to-date information about the nature, extent, causes, and consequences of cyberbullying among adolescents.
Visit: www.Cyberbullying.us

Don't Believe the Type is an Internet prevention website for teens on identifying sexual exploitation online.
Visit: tcs.CyberTipLine.com/KnowTheDangers.htm

Federal Bureau of Investigation—Cyber Tip Line is the site for reporting unusual e-mail or Internet communication.
Visit: www.CyberTipLine.com

GetNetWise is a public service developed by a wide range of Internet industry corporations and public interest organizations.
Visit: www.GetNetWise.org

GLSEN is also a great organization that is working to eradicate bullying and bias in schools.
Visit: www.GLSEN.org

GuestAssist delivers student support for schools using mobile messaging technology.
Visit: www.GuestAssist.net

I Keep Safe is a broad partnership of governors and first spouses, attorneys general, public health and educational professionals, law enforcement, and industry leaders working together for the health and safety of youth online. IKeepSafe® uses these unique partnerships to disseminate safety resources to families worldwide.
Visit: www.IKeepSafe.org

i-SAFE—Internet Safety Education is a non-profit foundation for internet safety education.
Visit: www.iSafe.org

It Gets Better Project helps the many LGBT youth who can't picture what their lives might be like as openly gay adults. They can't imagine a future for themselves. So let's show them what our lives are like, let's show them what a future may have in store for them.
Visit: www.ItGetsBetter.org

The Megan Meier Foundation raises awareness, educates, and promotes positive change to children, parents, and educators in response to the ongoing bullying and cyberbullying in our children's environment.
Visit: www.MeganMeierFoundation.com

The National Center for Bullying Prevention is helping to promote awareness and teaches effective ways to respond to bullying.
Visit: www.Pacer.org/bullying

The National Cyber Security Alliance provides tools and resources to empower home users, small businesses, and schools, colleges, and universities to stay safe online.
Visit: www.StaySafeOnline.org

NCSL (National Conference of State Legislatures) lists state laws regulating online behavior or use of electronic devices.

For state laws regarding electronic communication devices on school property:

Visit: www.ncsl.org/default.aspx?tabid=17853

For state laws regarding computer harassment or cyberstalking laws:

Visit: www.ncsl.org/IssuesResearch/
TelecommunicationsInformationTechnology/
CyberstalkingLaws/tabid/13495/Default.aspx

Netsmartz is committed to keeping kids and teens safer on the Internet.

Visit: www.NetSmartz.org/Teens

Visit The Kids Site (also a good example of using games for learning).

Visit: www.NetSmartzKids.org/indexFL.htm

The One-Click Audio Series provides parents with the complete program and information to stop online and textual harassment. This seven-disc series is full of interviews, discussions, and answers you need about the dangers of social networking and how to parent in our digital world.

Visit: www.oneclicksafetykit.com

The "One-Click Safety Kit" helps parents defend against sexting, cyberbullies, and textual harassment by providing parents with a turnkey program that helps avoid online dangers and helps you negotiate with your children *before* they get access to technology. The kit comes complete with contracts, warning notices, social networking rules to live by, resources and support, and definitions of terms that you need to know. It's a must-have for every parent with children between the ages of eight and eighteen.

Visit: www.oneclicksafetykit.com

STOMP Out Bullying is focused on reducing bullying and cyberbullying.

Visit: www.StompOutBullying.org

Stop Bullying Now! is here to help you stop bullying in your school and community.

Visit: www.StopBullyingNow.com

Teenangels are a group of thirteen- to eighteen-year-old volunteers who have been specially trained in all aspects of online safety, privacy, and security. After completion of the required training, the Teenangels run unique programs in schools to spread the word about responsible and safely surfing the web to other teens and younger kids, as well as parents and teachers.

Visit: www.TeenAngels.org

The Trevor Project is a twenty-four-hour national help line for gay and questioning teens. The hotline is 866.4U.TREVOR.

Visit: www.TheTrevorProject.org

Wired Safety provides help, information, and education to Internet and mobile device users of all ages, handling cases of cyber abuse ranging from identity and credential theft, to online fraud and cyber stalking, to hacking and malicious code attacks. It is a cyber-neighborhood watch and operates worldwide in cyberspace through more than 9,000 volunteers worldwide.

Visit: www.WiredSafety.org

The Parent's Guide
Product Information

Shawn Edgington's

ONE-CLICK
SAFETY KIT

Online Harassment

Keep your children safe and secure online. Be proactive against phone and Internet usage, sexting, cyberbullying, online predators, and textual harassment by using the One-Click system.

One-Click is a formalized turnkey system for parents with children who have cell phones and/or access to the Internet and who want to set rules for usage and avoid online dangers from occurring. You'll be provided with:

The Cell Phone and Social Media Contract
- ✓ The "Rules of Engagement" contract
- ✓ Twenty talking points about the dos and don'ts for your child's online and cell phone activity
- ✓ An action plan that's ready to implement when rules are broken
- ✓ Formal written warning notices (first through fourth offense)
- ✓ Formal termination of technology notice
- ✓ Agreement to be signed and dated by child and parents

Talking Points, Programs, and Resources
- ✓ Description of terms and need-to-know information about the technology you'll be addressing with your children
- ✓ The ten Facebook rules for parents to live by
- ✓ Consequences of sexting and "sextortion"
- ✓ The warning signs of textual harassment
- ✓ The importance of setting clear boundaries

Cell Phone Only Contract
- ✓ The "Rules of Engagement" contract
- ✓ An action plan that's ready to implement when rules are broken
- ✓ Covers calls, texting, and data usage
- ✓ Formal written warning notices (first through fourth offense)
- ✓ Formal termination of cell phone notice
- ✓ Agreement to be signed and dated by child and parent

Social Networking & Internet Only Contract
- ✓ The "Rules of Engagement" contract
- ✓ An action plan that's ready to implement when rules are broken
- ✓ Covers social networking sites and Internet usage
- ✓ Formal written warning notices (first through fourth offense)
- ✓ Formal termination of Internet and social networking sites
- ✓ Agreement to be signed and dated by child and parent

BONUS Material:
- ✓ The Ignore/Block/Report Program
- ✓ Why a "parental controls" service is a must for your child's wireless number
- ✓ The Cyberbullying Report
- ✓ The importance of setting boundaries and consequences with your children

*All documents are completely editable, which allows you the freedom to make the changes that best fit your family's needs.

One-Click Safety Kit - Copyright 2010

For more information, visit:
www.OneClickSafetyKit.com

One-Click Safety Kit

The One-Click Safety Kit was created from extensive research, personal experience, professional knowledge, and advice from professionals in the field of safety and loss prevention. You now have instant access to a turnkey system that really works. By using the pre-developed contracts, forms, warning notices, and resources included with the One-Click system, you can help your family set boundaries and expectations regarding appropriate cell phone and Internet usage.

According to recent surveys:

➤ On a daily average, 160,000 children miss school because they fear they will be bullied if they attend classes.

➤ On a monthly average, 282,000 students are physically attacked by a bully each month.

➤ Every seven minutes a child is bullied on a school playground; over 85 percent of those instances occur without any intervention.

➤ Almost 50 percent of teens admit to being harassed online or by text message.

➤ As a result of being bullied, 19,000 children attempt to commit suicide over the course of one year.

With the One-Click system, you can be proactive—instead of reactive—against phone and Internet usage.

Shawn Edgington's

ONE-CLICK
AUDIO SERIES

Online Harassment

The One-Click Audio Series provides awareness and solutions for parenting in today's digital world. Knowledge is power! If you're aware of what's happening, you can take action, get involved, and facilitate change.

- -

The One-Click Audio Series provides awareness, solutions, and preventative resources you can use.
With defensive parenting and constant communication, you can teach your children about the potential dangers of social networking, empower them to protect themselves from online predators, guard their personal information, preserve their online reputation, and learn how to determine friends from "frenemies." The One-Click Audio Series discusses:

Disc #1: Parenting Around Technology
- ✓ Why parenting around technology is important and what proactive steps you can take to help keep your children safe and secure while they are online
- ✓ What the Ignore/Block/Report Program is, how to use it, and why it's critical
- ✓ What the warning signs of textual harassment are and what you can do to stop harassment if it's occurring
- ✓ How to teach important techniques to your child—the cornerstone of social networking and text message survival
- ✓ Text message monitoring tools and the importance of parental controls

Disc #2: Facebook 411
- ✓ The importance of monitoring the "right way"
- ✓ How Facebook privacy and places settings work
- ✓ The ten Facebook rules to live by
- ✓ Why it's important to monitor your child's "friends"
- ✓ An in-depth interview with a parent who monitors her children's social networking sites daily as she discusses the right way to monitor your teens on Facebook
- ✓ How to empower your child to "block" on Facebook

Disc #3: The Rules of Engagement
- ✓ How to execute the Rules of Engagement contract and why it's important
- ✓ How to be proactive when it comes to your child's cell phone and Internet usage
- ✓ Important terms and terminology so you know what to be concerned about and what to watch for

Disc #4: The Cyberbullying Epidemic
- ✓ What cyberbullying is and what you can do about it
- ✓ The profile of a cyberbully and the ten warning signs to watch for
- ✓ The steps you can take if you find out your child is a cyberbully
- ✓ How to be proactive and empower your child to defend against a cyberbully
- ✓ An in-depth interview with a mother who experienced the wrath of a cyberbully

Disc #5: Importance of Online Branding and Reputation Management
- ✓ How to protect your child's online image and reputation
- ✓ Why teens get into trouble online and how you can help avoid it
- ✓ Who is really watching you on and offline and the safeguards you can take to limit exposure
- ✓ How to identify online predators

Disc #6: Sexting and Sextortion 911
- ✓ What sexting and sextortion are
- ✓ How it happens and what you can do to limit your child's risk
- ✓ What monitoring tools are available and the consequences of sexting
- ✓ An in-depth interview with a parent who learned sexting the hard way

Disc #7: Cyberbullying and Online Harassment in Our Schools
- ✓ What parents need to know about the fast-paced digital world
- ✓ An in-depth interview with a principal who installed a state-of-the-art student support system using text messaging
- ✓ What you can do to help keep your child safe and secure while they are at school

**A bonus disc is included with more interviews and important information about
understanding the benefits and dangers of parenting in a digital world.**

One-Click Safety Kit - Copyright 2010

For more information, visit:
www.OneClickSafetyKit.com

One-Click Audio Series

The One-Click Audio Series provides awareness and solutions for parenting in today's digital world. Knowledge is power! If you're aware of what's happening, you can take action, get involved, and facilitate change. Within this eight-disc series, you'll learn:

➢ Why you as a parent must understand today's technology for your children to stay safe and secure online.

➢ How to empower your children to defend against textual harassment, sexting, online predators, "sextortion," and cyberbullying.

➢ Why you need to execute a formalized "Rules of Engagement" contract for your child's social media and cell phone usage and set boundaries.

➢ How to protect your teen's online image and reputation and how to monitor your teen's Facebook account.

➢ Everything about cyberbullying, including an interview with a parent who has experienced and confronted tragedy as a result of online harassment.

The One-Click Audio Series provides awareness, solutions, and preventative programs with tips you can use. With defensive parenting and constant communication, you can teach your children about the potential dangers of social networking, guard their personal information, empower them to protect themselves from online predators and preserve their online reputation.

Also available as an E-Book

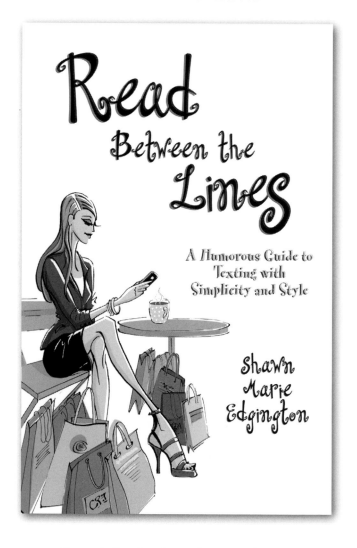

Shawn's first book, *Read Between the Lines*
is available at: www.ShawnEdgington.com
And wherever books are sold.

Get With It or Get Deleted

Read Between the Lines is perfect for the person who wants to improve or learn how to communicate instantly with anyone at any time, from just about anywhere. In ten short chapters, you'll learn how to:

- Improve daily communication across generations
- Tweet on Twitter™
- Practice appropriate texting etiquette
- Keep up with teen texting and know what to watch out for
- Understand how educators and the hard of hearing use texting
- Use texting in an emergency situation

And much more!

Bottom Line: Whether you're in the bedroom or in the boardroom, on Main Street or on Wall Street, most of life's texting situations are covered in this fun and stylish text survival guide. You'll "BECOME A TEXPERT" in no time.

Quick Start Into Texting

G2G · Got To Go		**NP** · No Problem	
YTB · You're The Best		**STD** · Seal The Deal	
IDK · I Don't Know		**TWTR** · Twitter	
COT · Circle of Trust		**OTP** · On The Phone	
H&K · Hugs & Kisses		**OMW** · On My Way	

Shawn's first book, *Read Between the Lines* is available at: www.ShawnEdgington.com And wherever books are sold.

The Parent's Guide is
also available as an Audio Book

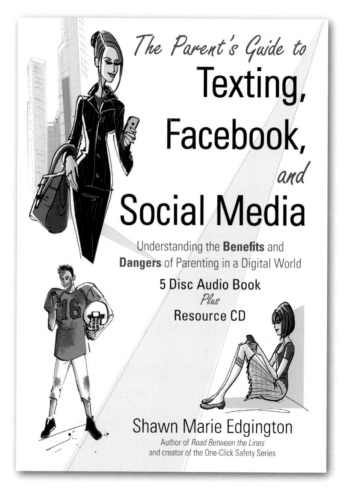

For more information, visit:
www.ShawnEdgington.com

Read Between the Lines iPhone Apps

"OMG!" and "LOL" are the ultimate text lingo diction-
aries that allow you to figure out what the heck your
BFFs are trying to say. Discover hot new (and cool old)
abbreviations, making it easier for you to say more—in
less. After all, isn't that the main reason you text? This
application delivers the texting lingo you need, where
you need it most—right into the palm of your hand.

> ➤ Explore new terms and keep your friends guessing

> ➤ Less is more—say what you want with simplicity
> and style

> ➤ Use new terms to add some humor to your messages

> ➤ Browse through thousands of text abbreviations

> ➤ Look up definitions in a snap

> ➤ Share your favorites on Facebook and Twitter

> ➤ Easy to use

> ➤ Fun and colorful design

Search Keywords: OMG, LOL, or "text lingo" in the
iTunes App Store or go to www.ShawnEdgington.com
to purchase for ninety-nine cents.

Cyber Safety Academy Fundraiser
Available for Schools and Organizations

The Cyber Safety Academy Fundraiser offers parents, educators, counselors and children multiple ways to become cyber-safe across a multitude of platforms:

➤ Books

➤ Workbooks and Instructor Guides

➤ Parental Internet Monitoring Software

➤ Educational DVD's and CD's

➤ And much more

Raise awareness and funds by offering the Cyber Safety Academy Fundraiser as an alternative to wrapping paper, cookie dough or candy within your organization.

For more information, visit:

www.CyberSafetyFundraiser.com

About the Author

Shawn Marie Edgington is America's leading "Texpert" and cyberbullying prevention expert. She's the author of *Read Between the lines: A Humorous Guide to Texting with Simplicity and Style*, the creator of the One-Click Safety Series, and a change management speaker. Shawn is the CEO of a national insurance firm located in northern California, where she provides risk management and guidance to clients across the country about the repercussions of inappropriate social media and harassment usage in the workplace.

After a personal experience she had with her sixteen-year-old daughter being threatened by text and on Facebook, she has made it her mission to provide parents with solutions that they can use to empower their children to defend against the daily threats they receive as a result of living in our ever-changing digital world.

Shawn has developed the One-Click Safety Kit, a turnkey system that's filled with tools to help families defend against sexting, cyberbullies, online predators, and textual harassment. Shawn is on a mission to help protect our kids against the dangers that exist on the wild, wild web, and wants every parent to know that no child is immune.

Shawn has been profiled on the Fox Business Channel, *Imus in the Morning*, *View from the Bay*, KRON 4 News, *The San Francisco Chronicle*, Fox News Radio, CBS Radio, *The Leslie Marshall Show*, *InfoTrak*, *The John Carney Show*, *Mom's the Word*, *The San Diego Union*, *American Cheerleader Magazine*, CNN Radio, NPR, and various other media outlets and syndicated radio programs across the country.

Shawn is not just a mom whose child was bullied. She is an expert that's been invited to speak about these topics at conferences and events around the country. Shawn provides awareness and solutions to parents and teens on how to take the steps to prevent social and mobile networking from turning into every parent's nightmare.

Shawn lives in the San Francisco Bay Area and is passionate about her family and helping others. Meet her or learn more about *The Parent's Guide*, *Read Between the Lines*, and her One-Click Safety Series, or share your personal story, at www.ShawnEdgington.com.